ATOM AND ORGANISM

ATOM AND ORGANISM

A NEW APPROACH
TO THEORETICAL BIOLOGY

BY WALTER M. ELSASSER

PRINCETON, NEW JERSEY

PRINCETON UNIVERSITY PRESS

1966

574
EL7a
84767
Sept 1973

PREFACE

The reader, especially since he is as likely as not quite a busy man, will want to be told in a few sentences what constitutes the "new approach" of the title. We shall try to do this, although much effort has gone into simplifying our exposition so as to keep the text as a whole to a limited size. The main proposition of this book is as follows: The time-honored dualism of the mutually exclusive systems of thought, mechanistic biology on the one hand and vitalism on the other, expresses a pair of theoretical approaches which are both inadequate. We shall show how they can be replaced by an abstractly descriptive system of a different type that is far better adapted to the nature of biology. There are good historical reasons for the past polarization of thinking in terms of this ancient dualism. For one thing, students of biology have been overawed by the stupendous advances of physical science; secondly it is clear that the study of physiology and also biochemistry invariably starts with a straightforward application of physical science, a basic fact to which we need to revert time and again. It does not at all follow that this must remain consistently so as one advances toward an understanding of organisms at a deeper level. But it is clear that if we started from mechanism or vitalism as alternative hypotheses, there would be a radical lack of symmetry between them; we need to investigate the character of this asymmetry in detail in order to appreciate the nature of the innovations required. Vitalism has in fact become a "dirty word" in many circles. This is not what keeps us from using it, but rather the fact that if we should try to hold on to it, we would soon be forced to change it beyond all recognition.

Our arguments will be strictly along the lines which

the modern scientist designates as positivistic. Lest the reader think that we are too emphatically concerned with philosophy proper, we let Alfred Whitehead (1957) speak for us: "The modern account of nature is not, as it should be, merely an account of what the mind knows of nature; but it is also confused with an account of what nature does to the mind. The result has been disastrous both to science and to philosophy, but chiefly to philosophy. It has transformed the grand question of the relation between nature and the mind into the petty form of the interaction between the human body and mind." Perhaps in some remote future the mind-body problem in this narrower sense will be restored to a central position, but certainly not before layer after layer of intervening problems pertaining to biology in a far more restricted sense have been thoroughly elucidated.

But to come back to earth, the conditions which any biological theory worthy of the name must satisfy are extreme. They are also more stringent at the present time than they may have appeared in the past. In the first place, there is no evidence at all that the basic laws of atomic and molecular physics (quantum mechanics) show any difference in the living organism as compared to inorganic matter. Also, one can no longer seriously doubt that life on our planet has arisen gradually from inanimate materials. Any design for a biological theory which does not allow these conditions or their consequences to be fulfilled in an altogether natural and not just in a contrived way ought to be discarded at once. We might think at first that these severe restrictions lead us of necessity into mechanistic preconceptions. The basic aim of this book is to demonstrate that this is not so. Within the theoretical scheme here presented the aforementioned requirements can certainly be fulfilled without difficulty, but we are bound to move far away indeed from conventional mechanistic thinking.

Throughout this book we lean quite heavily on the modes of thought of some modern branches of theoretical physics, especially atomic theory—but only by analogy. We are not primarily concerned with specialized deductive applications of the principles of quantum physics, but rather with a thorough conceptual analysis of the broader problems surrounding such applications. To illustrate, let us remember that before the advent of quantum theory, a wave theory and a corpuscular theory of light (the latter due to Newton) were considered to be mutually contradictory. Quantum mechanics has taught us that these two theories can be construed as two different and no longer contradictory aspects of reality; the dominance of either of these aspects is relative and depends on the method of observation. Niels Bohr pointed out, first in 1933, that physicists discovered here a conceptual scheme of remarkable breadth and capable no doubt of further generalization, especially in biology. Physicists and chemists have in the meantime concentrated their attention upon deductive applications of quantum theory to molecules and their interactions, with the greatest success, but they have paid far less attention to these wider conceptual questions. I hope that this book will be thought of as an elaboration and substantial extension of Bohr's germinal ideas. (The passionate interest of Niels Bohr in these problems is no accident; he told me once shortly before his death that his father was a physiologist and that he practically "grew up" in the biological laboratory.)

Since my book is concerned with questions of theory formation it cannot go into the detailed problems that make up the meat of biology. But as I am by training a theoretical physicist and have worked in fields that are not part of biology, I had to acquire, in one form or the other, a suitable background of concrete knowledge in biology. By sheer practical necessity the growth of my biological understanding was very gradual, extending over many years and coming at a much later age than is usual. In the end this turned out to be quite a good approach for the particular purpose because, as my understanding progressed, I was able to check every step carefully against the modes of thought and the established principles of physics. The fields of special concern were atomic and molecular physics and statistical mechanics. In these subjects I feel myself to be enough of a professional not to be readily led astray. Moreover this small book is the latest of a by now fairly lengthy series of publications on the subject. I hope that the progress achieved will be evident to those of my colleagues who have followed some of the earlier work.

It would be impossible to name all those biologists who over the years generously helped my understanding of their multifarious subjects. I would like to mention specifically my old friend, Dr. Th. Cahn of the Institut de Biologie in Paris, who many years ago first introduced me to the marvels and mysteries of biology. During the writing of this book, members of the Princeton Biology Department have been most helpful and encouraging; in particular Professor John Bonner gave unstintingly of his assistance and advice. I am greatly indebted to the Office of Naval Research for support of the research that ultimately led to this book and in particular to Dr. M. Garstens of its Physics Branch. Finally, I wish to acknowledge the help of the Humanities Council of Princeton University, which, by providing me with a Fellowship setting me free from some other duties, enabled me to complete the work.

WALTER M. ELSASSER

Guyot Hall
Princeton University
March 1966

CONTENTS

ATOM AND ORGANISM

CHAPTER 1 · STATEMENT
OF BASIC PRINCIPLE

1 · 1

On comparing the life sciences with the physical sciences we are immediately struck by the vastly greater complexity of their subject matter and by the lack of a deductive or otherwise precise theoretical structure. Such theoretical structure has always existed to some degree in physical science and has become strengthened as its branches grew. In particular the discoveries of atomic physics and the development of quantum theory have put a bottom under almost all parts of the physical sciences, and their structural organization and unification have grown apace in the course of this century.

Many students of biology have tried to achieve a systematization and unification after the pattern of physical science. These men have often expressed the view that once the "laws of biology" are discovered, a coherent edifice is bound to arise in which the particulars stand in about the same relationship to the fundamental laws as, say, chemistry or solid-state physics stand to basic quantum theory. Even if this be admitted as an abstract ideal it is most likely that the deviations from it will turn out to be so radical as to warrant our dismissing the idea that biology will ever become simply a sort of "superphysics." A different conceptual approach is needed, and it must of course be justified by empirical arguments. However, to simplify the task of the conceptual analysis attempted here we shall start from some fairly general ideas and proceed later to observational facts and concrete models. This procedure is meant to supplement the labors of those numerous natural philosophers of biology who have already traveled in the opposite direction.

We shall say at once that we accept basic physics as completely valid in its application to the dynamics of organisms. No modifications of either quantum theory or the second law of thermodynamics are contemplated. The fact that quantum theory, and hence chemistry, is the same *in vivo* as *in vitro* seems to agree with all known observational data and needs no detailed justification. The validity of the second law of thermodynamics in the organism has been doubted by some rather distinguished biologists. The matter is too complex to be treated at once; we shall return to some of the arguments later. Still, we must clearly be prepared to find that general laws of biology which are not deducible from physics will have *a logical structure quite different from what we are accustomed to* in physical science. The possibility of laws of biology which are "not deducible" from physics constitutes the center of our inquiry, and we shall try to clarify and define this concept as we proceed.

1 · 2

To facilitate our exposition we shall first introduce a plausibility argument: We claim that biology ought to be an *open* science to a much higher degree than physics is, the latter being more nearly a closed science by comparison. Now by an open science we emphatically do not mean a science of "open systems" in the technical sense, where an open system is one in which there is an inflow or outflow of matter, or of energy, or of both. The circumstance that nineteenth-century physical science limited itself mainly to closed systems and that the dynamics of open systems has been systematically studied only in fairly recent times, cannot detract from the fact that open systems as such are simply objects of physical science. Although all organisms are clearly open systems, we reject at this point the arbitrary assumption that open science can eventually be reduced to a science of open systems; in fact we shall see that this is not so.

Modern biology has clearly demonstrated that if we start from the simplest of organisms and go upward on the evolutionary ladder there is no point where we meet an iron curtain and can say: "Let us stop here and first systematize which is below, before we proceed upward." As C. H. Waddington (1962, p.23) puts it very precisely: "What is most nearly entitled to be called fundamental biology? The end-points of biological analysis, such as genes and sub-genic units? Or the most highly developed relationships that living things exhibit, the processes of human civilization? There is, of course, no one-way answer to any of these alternatives in biology." He proceeds to say that this state of affairs produces a certain "tension" in the pursuit of biology, which he considers to be an altogether vitalizing factor.

We are not concerned here with the progress from the amoeba to physical and cultural anthropology and thence into history. We are concerned with the progress from the organic molecule to the living state, and here there is a vast gap. The living state might be construed for simplicity in terms of a cell. But again, the progression from the molecule to the cell has many formal similarities to the progression from the amoeba to man's civilizations. In both cases we see a higher and integrated dynamics superordinated in a very complicated way over a combination of systems with a lower but already fairly complex dynamics. In this sense *the biophysicist has at least as much to learn from the biologist* as the latter has learned from the physicist. One of the motifs of this little treatise is an effort of the more abstractly oriented physicist to learn from biology.

1 · 3

Historically there have been two radical and distinct steps forward in our understanding of biology in purely mechanistic terms. The first one is the synthesis of organic compounds *in vitro*, starting with Wöhler in 1828. It eventually led to the demise of vitalism, which had dominated much of biology since the days of William Harvey if not since Aristotle. At the end of the nineteenth century, Driesch tried to revive vitalism but in this respect was quite unsuccessful among biologists, and the movement soon disappeared.

The second radical advance occurred a century later as a result of the development of large-scale electronic feedback automata around the end of the Second World War. The subject of automata theory was introduced to the general public by Norbert Wiener, who used the term "cybernetics" in his well-known book of this title. Soon it appeared that a large variety of biological phenomena (particularly the nervous reflex, but also many others) could be much more systematically described on being subsumed under the general head of automata theory. There has been a very rapid growth of the application of automata theory (as well as of the closely related subject of information theory) to biology ever since. It is altogether clear, however, that automata theory in itself is a branch of physical science, and, no matter how impressive the new problems it can solve, it enters biology at the same conceptual level as, say, chemistry. (Precisely what is meant by this we shall see later.)

Clearly, one cannot hope to make really substantial

progress in biological theory before the most significant aspects of the pertinent *physical* theories are well understood. If this condition is not fulfilled, efforts at developing biological theory in a precise fashion are bound to fail. Such was the case before the development of automata theory. Given the capital importance which theoretical biology is sure to have once it succeeds in shaping itself into a satisfactory form, it is incumbent upon the theorist to try and try again every time a major advance in physical science is achieved. Automata theory represents such an advance. Without having the kind of phenomena analyzable by automata theory under intellectual control, as it were, it would be impossible to test the validity of a new working hypothesis such as we propose below. It is of course a gamble to decide whether or not physical science is at any point sufficiently matured to permit the making of hypotheses or generalizations that help to fill the gap between the inanimate and the living. The hypothesis to be propounded here is specifically meant to go beyond automata theory. Our direction will be from closed to open theory, and the theory of feedback automata, being a branch of generalized mechanics, is, as we shall recognize more clearly later, no more than a partial advance in our direction. After this digression, we now return to the matter of closed and open theories.

1·4

We shall explain the meaning of the term "closed theory," as introduced here, by an example from mathematics. A typical closed system of mathematical propositions is Euclidean geometry. All its theorems can be derived from a limited number of axioms by purely deductive reasoning. The system is therefore entirely specified by the axioms, together with the operational rules for the process of deduction. The number of theorems that can be proved is unlimited, and the proof proceeds in each case by strictly formal logico-mathematical operations (which can in fact be carried out by an electronic computer). One characteristic property of such an abstract system is that just about every reasonable question can be answered by either yes or no; it has a *binary answer*, as it is expressed in the language of information theory; that is, a given proposition is either true or false.

[We do not plan to write a mathematical essay, and so we make no effort to define the term "reasonable question," nor do we think that a discussion of Gödel's theorem is pertinent here; this theorem says in effect that no mathematical system is completely closed in the sense that every question has a unique answer; it will suffice here to look at the constructs of mathematics from a much more primitive viewpoint.]

Consider now as an alternate example the theory of probability. Although this is in some respects a more complex subject than geometry, its foundations are well established and a complete set of axioms was developed by Kolmogoroff. Still, the structure of this abstract system is quite different from the structure of geometry. On the one hand, there are quantitative laws. For instance, if we throw a coin a large number of times the ratio of heads to tails will approach unity; we can bring this ratio as close to unity as we wish by making the number of throws large enough (provided we are dealing with an ideal coin which is not "loaded"). On the other hand, we cannot make an accurate prediction for a small number of throws. We can only assign probabilities which do not specify the outcome exactly. Thus there exist very numerous, quite simple and reasonable questions *which do not have binary answers*. We shall now define an open system of propositions as one with this particular property. It seems clear on very general grounds that there can be various degrees of "openness" of an abstract system.

In mathematics as a rule (though not necessarily so) one studies propositions which have binary answers. In probability theory, this means that one deals with the numerical probabilities which are defined as frequencies of occurrence in *infinite* sets; one does not commonly think in terms of finite configurations except in so far as these can be subsumed under infinite sets, or repeated infinitely often. In our particular context we shall be interested in the openness of abstract systems, that is, in the presence of numerous questions for which there exist no quantitative answers. One usually tries to push unanswerable questions over the horizon, as it were, by doing the best at axiomatizing abstract systems; *here, we are looking in the opposite direction.* We are specifically searching for open systems of propositions in which there are many unanswerable questions; this in the hope, of course, that they will prove useful for theoretical biology.

1 · 5

Physics has for some generations now moved in the direction of more "openness." Celestial mechanics is the very model of a closed system of abstract theory where on the basis of Newton's laws, precise predictions are made starting from a limited number of astronomical observations. But kinetic theory (statistical mechanics) has an altogether different structure; it is an application of probability theory to the motion of molecules. Willard Gibbs, one of the founders of this science and a contemporary of the New England school of philosophical pragmatists, makes himself quite clear about the fact that ignoring the microscopic variables of individual molecules need not necessarily be an altogether "voluntary" act of renunciation. As opposed to Laplace, a century earlier, Gibbs leaves no doubt that once one introduces a "statistical model" of phenomena one must compare the model with the observations and one must determinedly disregard the temptation to speculate about the underlying individual molecular motion in the absence of specific evidence about the latter. His attitude is therefore strictly what in current language is called positivistic. (See the introduction to his book *Statistical Mechanics*.)

A further and even more radical step in the same direction came with the introduction of quantum mechanics. Here, statistical elements are an intrinsic feature of the theory; it is no longer possible, even ideally or abstractly, to separate the principles of the theory into two groups: rigorous laws of mechanics on the one hand and statistical assumptions on the other. Any interaction between electrons, protons, or other elementary particles involves statistical features. Only in terms of statistics can the wave-particle duality of quantum mechanics be given a consistent interpretation. In this sense quantum mechanics is very much an open theory: there are many questions (in fact most questions) to which the answers are in terms of probabilities only. Precise numerical values are then obtained only as limits for infinitely long series of samples, otherwise no binary or otherwise quantitatively definite answers exist. Since quantum mechanics has been the object of so much discussion and popular presentation it will suffice to mention these aspects of the science here without evoking further details. Another peculiarity of quantum theory, however, while no less fundamental, has been subjected to much less detailed study but is so important that we must go into it.

1 · 6

One of the most remarkable properties of atoms and of molecules of a given species is that they are *exactly alike*. This fact has of course been implicitly postulated and used by chemists for ages. Quantum mechanics goes one step further in showing that without the indistinguishability or quantitative identity of all electrons, chemical bonding as we know it would not be possible. It is of course not at all obvious that Nature should be thus constituted. We could conceive in principle of forms of matter where any two atoms are a little bit different from each other. If these differences were large enough the standard procedures of physics and chemistry would be very much altered. It would no longer be possible to look up, say, the melting point or the absorption spectrum of a chemically pure substance in a reference book and to apply these numbers to the experiment at hand. Instead, we might well be forced to measure these quantities anew for every sample. The reader may let his imagination roam to assess the consequences. In fact we are not so much interested here in the practical aspects as we are in the *logical* situation, since we are concerned with scientific method, at least for the time being, and it is clear that any views about the structure of matter would look rather different depending on whether or not we are entitled to postulate the basic equality of its constituents.

[In actual practice a certain type of variation persists— that which arises from the existence of isotopes of atomic nuclei. We shall here disregard this particular variation. This will not affect in any significant way the conceptual arguments with which we are dealing, or any results of our analysis; merely, everything we have to say would have to be stated in a more involved and cumbersome way, to the detriment of the clarity with which we are able to exhibit the basic issues.]

Assume for instance that we have, say, a reservoir of helium gas. We pick out one atom (by letting it escape through a shutter), make some measurement on it, and then throw it back into the reservoir. After a while we pick out another atom. It is then true, and quantum mechanics specifies this in the most precise mathematical terms, that we cannot tell whether the second atom is the same object we had the first time or some other one of the atoms in the reservoir. *The concept of individuality loses all operational meaning.*

Combine this now with the fact that, according to quantum mechanics, measurements in the atomic realm yield only statistical results. For instance, if we want to measure the distance between the orbital electron and the nucleus in the hydrogen atom, we obtain, not a fixed distance, but a statistical result, a probability distribution. Notice now how this combines with the fact that individual atoms are indistinguishable from each other. Except for this rigorous indistinguishability no exact meaning could be attributed to a purely statistical distribution of properties of atoms and molecules. These two properties supplement each other; more precisely, the property of being indistinguishable possessed by atoms and molecules is a necessary requisite of our being able to interpret the results of measuring processes in an exact probabilistic fashion, as quantum mechanics requires.

It is clear, then, that the meaning of statements in quantum mechanics is quite different from the meaning of statements in "classical" mechanics. On the basis of

Newtonian mechanics we can make many mathematical statements about planetary systems in general, but when it comes to specific measurements they refer to an individual planetary system such as our own. The situation in quantum mechanics is quite different. Apart from some very specialized limiting cases, into which we need not enter here, the statements of quantum mechanics refer essentially to *classes* of objects. Owing to the rigorous equality of atoms and molecules all statements about individual systems are implicitly statements about a class. This would be far less relevant than it is, except for the fact that statements in quantum mechanics are as a rule statistical and hence the exact equivalence of the members of a class is necessary for the theory to have a precise meaning at all. This fact has also found its deposit in scientific language. *When the quantum mechanician speaks of a "system" he always denotes a class.* This is so commonplace as to have become almost unconscious, although clearly it deserves analysis. As we shall see, the problem of relating theoretical biology to theoretical physics centers about the relationship of individual and class, in a sense to be elucidated as we go on.

This argument stands in need of one additional refinement. Atoms and molecules can exist in a variety of quantum states. The higher quantum states are as a rule comparatively short-lived and go over into the ground state, usually with emission of a quantum of radiation. Within the conceptual framework of quantum mechanics, however, each state can be considered as a separate entity. Two atoms are fully equivalent only if they are in the same quantum state. The concept of a set of atoms or molecules of identical composition and all in the same quantum state is one commonly employed in quantum theory (where it is called a "pure state," which term, again, puts in evidence the non-distinction between individual and class). Two objects of quantum theory composed of equivalent nuclei, having the same number of electrons, etc., and being in the same quantum state are utterly indistinguishable. A large number of indistinguishable objects of this kind is required to verify the statistical predictions of the theory. Such a set of atoms or molecules, each having the same composition and all being in the same quantum state, will be denoted as a *fully homogeneous class*. Other classes of objects of atomic and molecular physics will be designated as inhomogeneous; we shall also speak of classes that are more or less homogeneous, the meaning of this somewhat looser language being obvious.

1 · 7

Looking back, then, we see that we are confronted with a rather surprising development. Modern physics, or much of it, deals not so much with objects as it does with homogeneous classes, where one member of the class is completely substitutable for the next. We think that much if not most of the gulf that still yawns between the physics of biomolecules and biology proper results from the conceptual difficulties which arise when observational material as inhomogeneous as that of biology is forced into the mold of a conceptual scheme which is too narrow for it.

Radical inhomogeneity is by universal consent an outstanding and altogether basic property of all the phenomena of life. The proposition "no two cells are ever exactly alike," often enunciated by observing biologists, summarizes a vast amount of empirical evidence. It is not the expression of some vague poetic feeling about Nature but the condensation of the result of innumerable sharp-eyed observations. Moreover, it is a property to be found at all levels of biological organization. That humans have individuality and that the shepherd can tell his sheep apart is hardly news. The adage that "no two blades of grass are ever alike" represents a generalization of very considerable age. It was a principle of medieval philosophy, and we trust that some knowledgeable historian will be able to trace it to Aristotle or beyond. Apparently the founders of modern science in the seventeenth century were much exercised by this kind of thought. It has always been considered strange that Descartes denied the existence of atoms and tried to develop a pure continuum theory of matter, and this in the face of the heavy weight of the Renaissance tradition harking back to Lucretius, who explained everything by atoms. The attitude becomes far more intelligible if one notes Descartes' quandary: The principle that no two blades of grass are ever alike, he says, contradicts the existence of atoms. If one remembers that to Descartes "blades of grass" must have been practically a synonym for infinity, his line of thought appears altogether well founded. How can one construct an infinite variety of blades of grass out of a finite bundle of atoms? Needless to say, he radically overestimated the size of atoms and radically underestimated the magnitude of the numbers of combinatorics—the number of ways in which objects can be arranged to give different patterns. Again Pascal, the founder of probability theory, has an altogether similar concern: Organic life, he says, is inserted into inorganic nature in such a way that the former is of negligibly small extent compared to the latter. Most likely, the same quandary that puzzled Descartes must have been in the back of his mind.

After the discovery of Newtonian mechanics the role of organic life as a primary phenomenon receded somewhat into the background of prevalent philosophical thought. There now appears the problem of *compatibil-*

ity: How can the existence of organisms be reconciled with the existence of strict mechanical casuality of the Newtonian pattern? Leibniz, in his older age, preoccupied with philosophical problems, offers a highly original solution. The organism, he says, is an automaton throughout, but it differs from man-made automata in that there are, in "natural automata," wheels within wheels, automata within automata, in infinite regression. Evidently, the infinite regression which he postulates prevents the contradiction between the existence of organisms as autonomous units on the one hand and mechanical causality on the other. In spite of their brilliance, Leibniz' views on this point found little acceptance, owing to their rather obvious artificiality.

1 · 8

The starting point for a modernization of these ideas is found in the fact that at the base of our present-day understanding of atomic and molecular mechanics there are two pervasive concepts. One is the notion of homogeneous classes; it has been briefly discussed and we shall revert to it again. The other basic idea underlying quantum mechanics is that a measuring process in the realm of the elementary constituents of matter represents a physical interaction which produces a non-negligible disturbance of the system to be measured. If we observe a planet, the light which is used for the observation does not deflect the planet measurably from its orbit. But if we want to determine the location of an electron in an atom or molecule by means of radiation of sufficiently short wavelength, say X-rays, there occurs what is suitably described as a collision between the electron and the quantum of radiation; in a calculable fraction of the cases the electron will be "knocked out" of its orbit as a result of the collision. Quantum mechanics tells us that a disturbance of this type is intrinsically inevitable if the measurement is made in atomic dimensions. This of course is inseparable from the fact that the determination of position in the atomic realm can only be statistical; one can assign to the electron only a statistical "wave function," not a precise individual location.

Beginning in 1933 Niels Bohr applied these ideas to the investigation of the molecular structure of organisms. He coined the term *generalized complementarity* to describe his scheme: If we try to predict with precision the future behavior of an organism we must, according to physics, know the *initial values* of the positions and velocities of its constituent particles with sufficient accuracy. It might not be necessary to measure all of these at exactly the same moment, but they ought to be measured during some limited initial interval. If we cannot collect this precise information, prediction of the future behavior of the system becomes correspondingly limited. Now even in a relatively simple organism, a cell say, there are billions of orbital electrons which maintain a most intricate system of chemical bonds. The vital activity of the cell, especially metabolism, consists exactly in the changing of bonds, in the transfer processes which these bonding electrons undergo as time goes on. But quantum mechanics tells us that in order to localize an electron to within a reasonable accuracy on the molecular scale, say to within one angstrom, a physical interaction of the electron with the measuring probe (e.g., X-rays) must take place which, *in the average*, transmits a certain amount of the interaction energy to the electron. Very simple calculations show that the average energy per measuring process is by no means negligible compared to the average bonding energy. Thus if we admit multiple measuring processes even as an idealization, a corresponding number of bonds will be dislocated or broken. In order to make valid predictions for an appreciable time ahead it would be necessary, in a system as complex dynamically and as interrelated as an organism, to determine quantitatively many if not most of the existing bonds. The energy conferred upon the tissue by virtue of the measurements becomes then so large that vast changes must take place: the system will be radically altered and disrupted and is no longer even approximately equal to the system which was at hand before the measurements were undertaken. It is quite safe to say that these disturbances as they become cumulative must be deleterious: the organism becomes non-viable and ultimately dies.

This is Bohr's view on the effect, upon a living system, of multiple measurements in the atomic realm. The argument is so directly based on the principles of quantum theory that it seems quite impossible to avoid these conclusions otherwise than by abrogating quantum mechanics, a step which would be utterly arbitrary. Notice, however, that Bohr *does not deal with classes*; he speaks specifically of an individual organism whose behavior we want to predict on the basis of measurements made during some initial time interval. Hence it is adequate prediction of the *individual organism*, based on measurements on that individual object, which becomes effectively impossible as we go from the conceptual-mathematical scheme of classical physics to that of quantum physics. The relationship to the concept of homogeneous classes cannot be clarified so simply because organisms in experience are not sufficiently well-defined objects on the molecular and atomic scale to be considered members of homogeneous classes in the sense of quantum mechanics. The biological classes of experience are inhomogeneous, and they would first have to be homogenized by a process of selection, which we shall consider a little later.

It is important here to be perfectly clear about one thing: Bohr's arguments have no basic reference to life as an empirical phenomenon in its own right; the essential reference is to the structural and dynamical *complexity* of living matter considered as a phenomenon of physics pure and simple. It could not very well be otherwise unless one wanted to end up with a dualistic biology. Bohr then concludes from the results of his analysis that life is a primary phenomenon which can only be observed in its manifestations not, as such, analyzed. In other words, he refuses to define life either in terms of physics or in terms contradicting physics. Using the terminology introduced above we can say that in Bohr's view the application of quantum mechanics to highly complex systems shows this theory to be much more *open* than one might have expected at first sight. Predictions about the individual system being most severely limited by virtue of the disturbances introduced by measurement, there are many questions about individual systems which do not possess answers in the quantum mechanics of complex systems; in order not to destroy the organism we are forced to limit our observations, and we must correspondingly limit our predictions in a fundamental manner.

[To digress for a moment into the philosophical attitude taken by Bohr, we are clearly not dealing with an altogether novel train of thought concerning the character of life. Among the older views we might quote those of Claude Bernard (1878) as an outstandingly lucid example. It is a natural tendency of the human mind, he says, to insist always on knowing the causes of phenomena. But there are first causes which are intrinsically inaccessible to us. Since life, he says, represents first and foremost creativity, the explanation of the basic nature of life would lead us into the study of first causes, which are beyond the scope of science. He quotes Newton as saying that he who concerns himself with first causes shows by this very fact that he is not a scientist. Science is concerned with secondary or proximate causes, and the laws of physics and chemistry represent such proximate causes. Bernard most emphatically states that there can be no deviation at all from the laws of physics and chemistry in the organism. He tells us again and again that physics and chemistry must ultimately be able to explain every detail in the functioning of the organism, but at the same time they cannot explain its existence. Similar views were expressed by contemporaries of Bernard who combined physiology with philosophical interests, especially Lotze and Fechner.]

As Bohr's analysis shows, the whole approach to the relationship of biological to physical theory has become radically changed due to developments in atomic and molecular physics and chemistry which became crystallized in the laws of quantum mechanics. One fact, however, must not be overlooked, namely, that the problem with which we are concerned is of a type quite different from the study of, say, nuclei or large biomolecules. It is of a piece with some of the traditional philosophical preoccupations of mankind. This has two major consequences. In the first place, any study of the problem is beset by all kinds of emotional involvements and complexities, which is no more than what one must expect in a field of thought of this particular type. This state of affairs is obviously not such as to make the task of the investigator easier. In the second place, the problem lies at the confluence of several special sciences. Specialists, by their very nature, tend to be selective. Philosophers on the other hand have always considered it their particular business to counteract the tendency of mental selection to which the practitioners of concrete sciences are often more exposed than the public realizes. If, therefore, we deal with the relationship of organic and inorganic matter we should relate ourselves to some degree to philosophy and to the continuity of the philosophical thought of the past. We could suitably apply an old maxim of the philosophers: After everything is said and done in philosophical analysis, the end result should not differ too violently from the short-cut solution offered by common sense, otherwise it might be philosophy rather than common sense which is suspect. Similarly here; we would do well to remain in touch to some degree with traditional philosophy. If the outcome of our inquiry is too much in contradiction with the somewhat intuitive results of traditional philosophy, it might not ultimately be tradition which is wrong. Bernard's view that neither vitalism nor mechanism can win a complete victory in their long drawn-out struggle seems only rational in this light.

1 · 9

A vastly closer and more satisfactory approach to the problem than the traditional one can be effected by recognizing that modern science through kinetic theory and quantum mechanics is moving in the direction of a *more open* logical structure. The more numerous the questions which are intrinsically unanswerable in physical theory and which *can be recognized and precisely defined as such,* within the framework of the established theory, the more likely it becomes that the traditional difficulties which surround our problem can be minimized. We shall now show that one can advance considerably beyond Bohr by a rather consistent generalization of his ideas within the accepted structure of physical theory, which we of course take as being equally applicable to organisms and to inorganic matter.

We first must voice one minor criticism of Bohr's theory which has nothing to do with its content but refers to his terminology. Bohr speaks of generalized complementarity; this term might well give the impression that one is dealing with a conceptual or mathematical modification of the principles of quantum theory. This is not the case. What Bohr does is to apply the well-known principles of quantum mechanics, which are described in the textbooks in terms of a single electron, proton, etc., to *systems* of a very high degree of complexity containing many electrons and nuclei. Bohr's ideas represent therefore essentially an *application* of the basic rules of quantum mechanics to systems of the degree of structural and dynamical complexity that are found in organic nature. In fact, any mathematical or formal-logical modification of the intrinsic content of quantum mechanics for purposes of biology would contradict the principle that there is no difference in the application of the laws of physics as between inorganic and organic matter. Of course little harm is done by terminology if it is clearly understood that Bohr's results are a necessary consequence of quantum mechanics as it stands without formal modification or logical generalization. It is like applying the laws of electrical conduction, not just to a single circuit element but instead to a very complex and elaborate network.

1 · 10

The author has tried for a long time to answer the question of whether one is able to say something more on the basis of general principles of quantum mechanics (as opposed to its innumerable special applications to the structure and dynamics of atoms and molecules). This search has led us to the *problem of the homogeneity of classes*, which is central to the interpretation of quantum mechanics, although it does not, as a rule, explicitly appear in the apparatus of the theory. Starting from here we shall show that the physical theory which underlies the description of organisms by means of quantum mechanics is even more open than one might be led to believe by a first survey. The writer first presented this approach in condensed form in his earlier book (1958, chapter 4) ; it is here considerably elaborated and forms the core of the present work.

The full import of the homogeneity of classes in quantum mechanics can be grasped only if one considers it in connection with the statistical features inherent in the theory. Certain basic physical characteristics of atoms and molecules, for instance the position of electrons relative to nuclei, can only be evaluated statistically; at the same time the measuring process produces disturbances which are also statistically distributed. Let us say once more, then, that the relationship between theory and observational practice can be stated only in terms of classes, otherwise it becomes effectively meaningless. This is to say that specimens of the same class are *substitutable* for each other in experimental procedures. Naturally, this is no more than a mathematical elaboration of what chemists have been assuming implicitly all along. A chemist who has a bottle of some chemically pure compound has not the slightest doubt that his specimen is just as good as the contents of a similar bottle in another chemist's laboratory. This fact takes on an enhanced importance in connection with the present inquiry, namely, the question as to what happens to this type of regularity in highly complex systems. Since Bohr tells us that the determination of the internal state of a complex system must remain utterly fragmentary if the system is a living one, it becomes necessary to look for a substitute for this lack of observational determinacy, and this substitute is given by the structure of atomic and molecular science itself; in a terminology which is fairly self-explanatory we shall call this the procedure of *measurement by sampling of classes*. Information gained by measuring some members of a class can be used to make predictions about the future behavior of other members of the class. In the limiting case which is capable of realization in the laboratory, this is the sampling of homogeneous classes. It is important to understand that this is not just a methodology invented for purposes of the chemist or physicist; instead, the methodology is patterned after experience, we are dealing with an inherent property of the empirical material. If a somewhat idealized observer of quantum mechanics makes measurements on the properties of an atomic species, helium atoms say, it is convenient to have the helium gas in a bottle in the laboratory, but this is not required. We could just as well imagine a series of observers placed around the solar system, or the galaxy for that matter, each observer measuring the characteristics of one or a few helium atoms. If these observers communicated their results to a central station by radio signals, the resulting statistical description of the properties of helium atoms would be *exactly the same* as that obtained on drawing all the atoms from a vessel in one laboratory. Hence we see that the method of measurement by sampling of a homogeneous class is not an incidental extension of the procedure applicable to an individual object; *it is an integral part of the measuring process in atomic and molecular physics and in fact an indispensable component of the entire scheme of atomic theory.*

We have said previously that a fully homogeneous class consists of objects which are not only chemically equivalent but which are also in the same quantum state. It should be intuitively clear that such a homogeneous class, if measured, gives us more precise information than an inhomogeneous class, a so-called mixture in which some atoms or molecules are in one quantum state, others are in other quantum states. This is formulated in quantum theory as a rigorous mathematical theorem: the fully homogeneous class corresponds to a state of *maximum definiteness of detail*; any class that is less homogeneous is less well defined in its detailed features, and hence any prediction of the future behavior of the class loses sharpness and accuracy when we go from fully homogeneous to mixed, that is, more or less inhomogeneous classes. A fully homogeneous class is, in quantum mechanics, the tool of *maximum predictability*. This is a fundamental fact to which we now must turn our attention inasmuch as prediction based on measurement of an individual object is so severely limited.

1 · 11

The question which confronts us here may at once be stated in a concrete manner. It is the problem of *homogenization by selection*. Although the meaning of this term is immediately apparent some examples are useful. The chemist clearly carries out a process of homogenization by selection if he purifies a substance in the laboratory by the removal of foreign species of molecules. The more he succeeds in this endeavor the more the class of molecules will be homogeneous with respect to chemical composition. It will, however, not in general be homogeneous with respect to the quantum states in which the individual molecules find themselves; if the molecules are not isolated from each other in a vacuum but are immersed in a temperature bath, there will be a statistical distribution of the molecules over a variety of quantum states. This holds at all temperatures except at the absolute zero-point of the temperature scale, where all the molecules will be in their ground state.

Quantum mechanics allows us to go one step farther: it tells us that, in principle at least, we can also separate the molecules with respect to their various quantum states. This procedure can be carried out in the laboratory in a few particularly favorable cases, especially in atomic beam experiments. Whenever this is done, pure homogeneous classes become available, and the quantitative predictions of the theory can be verified. However, the theory must go farther. Consistency requires that this isolation of homogeneous classes *be always possible*, at least in the form of some "Gedankenexperiment," an idealized process of preparing homogeneous classes. Notice in particular that in this we are not concerned with some more or less vague speculation; on the contrary. By assuming this possibility, we specifically limit the introduction of subsidiary hypotheses which would go beyond existing theoretical concepts; only thus are we in possession of a perfectly clearly defined *domain of verifiability* of the theory. This is a step of great philosophical importance. It is the equivalent in quantum mechanics, of the meta-scientific assumption so often made in the past for Newtonian mechanics, namely, that atoms, etc., are tiny balls whose positions and velocities can *in principle* be determined with any desired accuracy if we so desire. This determination permits prediction of the future behavior of the system with an accuracy corresponding to the accuracy of the initial measurements. For Newtonian mechanics, such a conception leads at once to the familiar contradiction between mechanical causality and any properties of organisms that one considers incapable of being understood in terms of this causality, that is, to the conflict between mechanistic and vitalistic philosophies.

The fully homogeneous class is, as we have said, the tool of maximum predictability in quantum mechanics. We are here of course less interested in concrete laboratory procedures for preparing homogeneous classes than we are in general operational rules that can be set up to describe the process of preparing such a class *in abstracto*. We shall state as one such rule that *homogeneous classes are obtained by selection of subclasses of an inhomogeneous class*. Such a process requires of course that we can observationally identify each member of the inhomogeneous class with respect to chemical composition and quantum state. Ignoring detailed procedures we just assume that such a process of selection is always possible. This corresponds to assigning to the theory the maximum domain of validity which it can possibly have; thus again, we make the conditions of our inquiry not easier but as hard as possible.

[One subsidiary assumption is required which does not constitute much of a restriction. We shall assume that each sample of any class, each material object, is confined to a finite volume of space and has finite energy. This harmless-looking requirement has an important mathematical consequence. It makes the number of quantum states of which the object is capable, *finite*. (A theorem of quantum mechanics says that a system enclosed in a finite volume of space and having finite energy has only a finite number of quantum states.) Now let N be the number of objects in the original inhomogeneous class and let N_1 be the number of objects in a suitably selected subclass. We define in the usual way the *probability* for any object which belongs to the larger class, to be also member of the smaller class by

$$p = N_1 \ / \ N$$

which is valid provided N is a sufficiently large number. We may assume that p is not zero, otherwise we can simply exclude from consideration those subclasses for which p vanishes, as they are not of physical interest. Furthermore, we can also assume safely that, for any subclass, p will be finite (i.e., not infinitesimal); this follows from the assumption made above that the number of states which the objects of the class are capable of assuming is finite; if we distribute objects over a finite number of states (each having a probability that is not zero) then each state will receive a number of samples that is a finite fraction of the total number of objects.

Having made these simple mathematical assumptions, we now let the number N of objects in the original class grow beyond all bounds, that is, we assume $N \to \infty$. It follows without difficulty, since p is finite by assumption, that the number of objects in the subclass also grows beyond all bounds, $N_1 \to \infty$. A class for which $N \to \infty$, may simply be called an *infinite class*.]

The result of the preceding mathematical argument can be stated thus: If the original class is infinite, then subclasses obtained by selection are also infinite. Now we assumed before that it is always possible to prepare more homogeneous classes by selection. We can go one step farther and apply the process of selection a number of times in succession, thus obtaining more and more homogeneous classes at each step. This series of selections must terminate when we have obtained a fully homogeneous class: it is an intrinsic property of a fully homogeneous class that all of its members are of identical structure, hence all of its subclasses are indistinguishable from the original class. The series of successive selections will terminate after a finite number of steps, since by assumption there is only a finite number of states to choose from.

The preceding arguments have been presented in a somewhat awkward fashion in order to avoid mathematical apparatus, but they can readily be made rigorous by using the mathematical tools of set theory. The reasoning indicated was first used in 1933 by J. von Neumann in a book containing the mathematical axiomatization of quantum mechanics and has since come into common usage. The basic conclusion drawn by von Neumann can now be readily grasped: Nothing prevents us from assuming that the classes of atomic and molecular physics are of infinite membership ideally speaking; hence we are entitled to assume that by a process of selection *we can always procure homogeneous classes of infinite membership.* The consequences and implications are far-reaching. It is no longer necessary to consider inhomogeneous classes by themselves; once all the homogeneous classes into which they can be analyzed have been prepared, one can simply go back to the inhomogeneous class by combining the homogeneous classes again in suitable proportions ("mixing" them is the technical term). The properties of the inhomogeneous class can readily be calculated once those of the homogeneous classes are known.

We noted previously that a fully homogeneous class corresponds to a maximum definiteness of detail within the objects which are the members of the class. Since inhomogeneous classes can always be reconstituted from their component homogeneous classes, it follows that it is legitimate to assume that one may ignore inhomogeneous classes except for matters of mere convenience. *In principle* it is possible to assume that homogeneous classes have been prepared and that all fundamental questions of theory may be evaluated in terms of these. To appreciate the physical significance of such a conclusion, let us recall our previous result that, in quantum mechanics, prediction can no longer be based on measurements made on an *individual* system (because the process of measurement itself alters the system) but, instead, the predictive process depends on our making measurements by *sampling of classes*. Now there is just one method that will allow us to give an actual physical significance to statistical prediction: that is to have enough equivalent copies of the object so that probabilities can be expressed operationally as *frequencies of occurrence, such frequencies being the only way of representing probabilities in a concrete, physical manner.*

The import of the preceding, seemingly abstract arguments should now become clearer. Since predictions based on measurement of an individual object are severely limited, the more so the more complex the system, it becomes indispensable that one should be able to procure *alternate copies* of the object at hand. If the object is very complex a very large number of such copies is required. If these copies are available, one can make measurements on all of them, and this will correspondingly increase the accuracy of the predictions. What we are saying can be expressed in other terms as follows. According to Bohr we must limit our measurements on a highly complex system such as one which we consider empirically to be alive. If we did not so limit the measurements we would kill the organism. But there exists an alternative. We can prepare a large class of strictly equivalent objects and divide this class into two parts. We treat one set of samples very gently so that they survive without being appreciably disturbed in their internal dynamics; we use the other set of specimens for measurements as thorough as we wish regardless of the destruction which this may produce. Quantum mechanics asserts that if the class has been homogeneous enough to begin with, it will be possible to use the samples measured (and destroyed) to make predictions about those samples which we permitted to survive. Two implications of this method are now readily recognized. In the first place the classes used for the purpose should be as homogeneous as possible; this ensures that one can obtain maximum definiteness of prediction. Hence the value of the postulate that fully homogeneous classes can always be procured. In the second place, if the objects to be studied are of an extremely complicated structure one clearly requires a vast number of equivalent specimens in order to secure detailed information under the limitations imposed on measurements by quantum mechanics. The postulate that infinite homogeneous classes can always be prepared protects one from the possibility that he might run out of specimens when the number required is extraordinarily large, which will be the case if dealing with extremely complex systems where only a tremendous number of measurements defines their internal state.

1 · 12

We come now to the core of our problem. Bohr tells us that we can know very little about the structure of an *individual* organism because we must restrict our measurements so that they do not dangerously interfere with the future functioning of the system. He does not consider the fact that an exhaustive set of measurement providing maximum definiteness of the predictions requires, according to the general precepts of quantum mechanics, that one measure the members of a *homogeneous class* of sufficiently large membership. The postulate that one can always procure such classes is suspect. Can one really do so? If not, predictability is curtailed even more than we might have expected, and we are obliged to move farther in the direction of an *open* theory. This represents the direction in which we shall go.

A very simple clarification of concepts is required first. An inhomogeneous class is one in which two samples (members of the class) are not in general alike. A homogeneous class is one in which any two members are fully or nearly alike; in a fully homogeneous class any two members are completely indistinguishable and substitutable for each other. For instance, the class of all helium atoms in their ground state is a fully homogeneous class. Now the term homogeneous is also used in a somewhat different sense. We speak of a homogeneous *system* (the word "system" standing here for a substance composed of atoms or molecules). Thus a volume of chemically pure helium gas confined within the walls of a vessel will in the ordinary language of the physicist or chemist be designated a homogeneous system. In general, the existence of homogeneous systems in this sense is a prerequisite for the preparation of homogeneous classes in the laboratory, since we cannot in general go around the universe with an atomic butterfly net as it were, to catch samples of a homogeneous class. There is then a logical distinction to be made between a homogeneous substance and a homogeneous class. It is not necessary to be pedantic and to introduce a new terminology provided one keeps the conceptual distinction in mind. As a rule, a homogeneous substance consists of molecules or atoms which, taken individually, form a homogeneous class.

Now let us look at organisms. They are utterly in-homogeneous in both senses of the word. They are of almost boundless structural complexity, and this is true of all autotrophic organisms known. At the same time, any class of organisms shows variability, that is inhomogeneity, of the class. The statement often heard by observing biologists, that no two cells are ever alike, and the older form of this, that no two blades of grass are ever alike, summarizes the facts, showing this in-homogeneity to be extreme. Now one might suspect that this inhomogeneity can be eliminated. Assuming that we have a sufficiently large assembly (class) of cells, we could select a subclass which is more homogeneous, and then select again to obtain an even more homogeneous sub-class, and so forth *ad infinitum*. But even simple cells constitute highly complex and heterogeneous systems, and the number of different patterns into which one can arrange the vast number of organic molecules, radicals, and electrons that go to make up a tissue the size of a cell is tremendous. Guesswork will not help here but only *actual calculations* pertaining to combinatorics. We shall later on be concerned with such calculations and shall here only anticipate the result: One finds that there are vastly more such combinations than one could possibly grow cells, even if all the surfaces of all the conceivable planets in the universe were covered with such organisms and were so covered for billions of years.

Nothing is gained, however, by hyperbolic, merely verbal propositions. This is a matter of calculation and, in addition, of interpretation. Take for instance an inorganic substance with some degree of inhomogeneity, such as a crystal composed of two types of atoms, which can intercrystallize freely (say silver and gold). One can readily calculate that even if a volume millions of light years in diameter were filled with crystal grains 1 micron in diameter, no two of them would be completely alike, meaning that in each lattice the way in which the silver atoms are distributed among the gold atoms, or conversely, would be slightly different. But the main point is that this is *irrelevant* in the case of the silver-gold alloy. All the significant physical properties of such a specimen are obtained by averaging over the individual atoms. After averaging, the details of the atomic arrangements will not in any significant way contribute to the final result. The same might be said of virtually all cases in which the properties of relatively homogeneous inorganic substances are related to their atomic or molecular constituents; this always takes the form of averaging, and in the averaging process the details of the atomic and molecular configurations will get lost.

This irrelevance of molecular arrangements for macroscopic results has given rise to the tendency to confine physics and chemistry to the study of homogeneous systems as well as homogeneous classes. In statistical mechanics a great deal of labor is in fact spent on showing that homogeneous system and homogeneous classes are closely related and to a considerable extent interchangeable concepts of theoretical analysis (Gibbs theory). Naturally, this is not an accident. The methods of physics and chemistry are ideally suited for dealing with homogeneous classes with their interchangeable components. But experience shows that the objects of biology are radically inhomogeneous both as systems (structurally) and as classes (generically). Therefore, the method of biology and, consequently, its results will differ widely from the method and results of physical science. *Inhomogeneity will be our key to the approach toward a theoretical treatment of biological phenomena.* We shall go so far as to say that we consider physics as the science dealing essentially with homogeneous systems and classes, and biology as the science of inhomogeneous systems and classes. As we go on, this distinction will be exhibited in more precise terms.

1 · 13

There is one point in the preceding system of abstractions which it would be very difficult to alter, that is the fundamental possibility of selecting subclasses of a given class. This possibility is so much inherent in the nature of science that one can see no way of changing it. Hence the value of our argument depends on the *success* of the procedure of selection. In actual practice, of course, there is no such thing as an infinite class. The use of infinite classes in the theory has nevertheless a well-defined operational meaning. We take the admission of infinite classes as the mathematical expression of the postulate that fully homogeneous classes can always be procured. This is in a sense the reverse of the logical situation usually described in scientific textbooks where the availability of infinite classes, without being explicitly discussed, is considered as self-evident, and the possibility of procuring fully homogeneous classes is, usually implicitly, derived from it. We readily see that from the viewpoint of the theory of classes this state of affairs represents a limiting case. The more general view would be that not all classes can be homogenized by selection. We shall now outline the abstract reasoning appropriate to theoretical biology as pertaining to a system of classes which represents *the opposite limiting case*: the investigator not only has difficulties in making the idealized assumption that he can always avail himself of a fully homogeneous class of objects; in the realm of living organisms he can, we assume, simply not do so. It is desirable to express this in a precise way. If an inhomogeneous class is of *finite membership,* the success of the procedure for obtaining homogeneous classes can no longer be guaranteed; we may quite simply *run out of specimens* during the process of selection before we have reached a point where an adequate homogenization in terms of a subclass has been achieved. We now assume that this will, in fact, always occur in organisms. Thus we are led to what might be called a non-Neumannian axiomatics, namely, one in which one postulates that all classes of objects of biology are finite, with the following implication. They are so limited in the size of their membership that the method of prediction based on sampling of classes becomes severely restricted. Consequently, as soon as we postulate the finiteness of classes we are faced with a *dual* restriction concerning the prediction of organisms: We cannot predict the individual because measurements on it of sufficient thoroughness are intolerable (Bohr), but we cannot now supplement this limited information by measuring *other members of the class* (which we are free to destroy) so as to apply the information gained in order to improve on the prediction of the system at hand. Naturally, this procedure does not become altogether impossible because, by the very nature of a class, its members have certain properties in common (members of a class of organisms as a rule have very many properties in common), and hence a partial prediction based upon the common properties of the members of the class can always be achieved. But if we probe deeper into details of structure, individual differences among members of the class will appear. Prediction is then simply limited by the fact that in a sufficiently inhomogeneous class we have no reason, in principle, to assume that two specimens are sufficiently alike in all their details; thus there is a limit to what sampling of classes can do for prediction. It may now readily be conceived that in the case of systems and classes as inhomogeneous as organisms these limitations can be vastly more far-reaching than they would be in the case of homogeneous substances. Hence a collection of finite and inhomogeneous classes corresponds to a type of science which is even more *open* in the sense defined previously than the homogeneous classes of atomic physics and of chemistry.

The postulate that classes have to be considered as finite in theoretical biology, not for the sake of a formal exercise but in order to prevent the concept of a fully homogeneous class from entering the theory of organisms, has been designated by the author (1958) as the *principle of finite classes.* All mathematical experience shows that the modification, the omission, or introduction of a single axiom leads as a rule to quite radical changes in the system of abstractions at hand. This is also the case here. Some implications of this change will be discussed in the following pages, although for obvious reasons we do not do this in a purely abstract manner. Having introduced irreducible inhomogeneity as a characteristic property of the classes of biology, we then return to the observational material in order to see whether we can better interpret the regularities of this material in an appropriate way without insisting at the present stage of the inquiry on an all too formal treatment. If the basic set of ideas is correct, it ought to find extensive application in theoretical biology as time goes on.

A further terminology is sometimes convenient. A set of abstractions in which all classes are finite (and some of them are radically inhomogeneous) will be designated as a *finite universe of discourse.* Its counterpart is, of course, the universe of discourse of classical physics where true limiting processes in the sense of mathematical analysis are always assumed possible. Clearly, the distinction is a purely ideological one, in the sense that in practice the number 10^{100} is indistinguishable from infinity. In spite of the familiar denials by some people who like to call themselves hard-boiled practitioners, we find that such abstractions may have a far-reaching influence on the art of formulating appropriate scientific concepts.

[So far as the homogeneity or inhomogeneity of classes is concerned, it is interesting to note that this has a remarkable counterpart in the history of Western philosophy. To see this, we need merely replace the concept of classes by the related one of the philosophers, that of universals. The discrepancy concerning the relative emphasis to be placed on universals as against individuals has pervaded many centuries of the older history of philosophy. It seems to have reached a peak in the long drawn-out controversy between the so-called realists and nominalists among the medieval scholastic philosophers. The realists claimed that the universals were more "real" than their representation by individuals, whereas the nominalists claimed that the universals were mere "names" for classifying individuals. As we have pointed out already, by the very nature of the problem an investigation of the type contemplated here must sometimes be as close to traditional philosophy as it is to physics and chemistry. Although moderns are more abstract and operational than philosophers of the middle ages, it is not to be wondered at that some of the problems and quandaries connected with inquiries into the nature of organisms are perennial. And it is hardly necessary to say again that no inquiry can afford to overemphasize radically one of these aspects at the expense of the other.]

1 · 14

Having spoken of the various conditions which make for a decrease of predictability in highly complex systems, we now pass to another facet of the problem. This will complete our enumeration of the effects which make the physics of organisms more of an open science than has hitherto been suspected. An organism is not only a physico-chemical system of an extraordinary degree of structural complexity; beyond this, its dynamics may often be represented in a good approximation by a feedback automaton with numerous interconnected feedback cycles. The dynamics of a cell consists of innumerable chemical reactions which are mediated by enzymes. The proteins, of which the enzymes are a most important class, are broken down, eliminated, and reconstituted in the metabolic process. Thus enzymes are both active agents and sometimes passive substrates of metabolic transformation; moreover, it is well known that enzymes can be deactivated by the presence of certain compounds and reactivated by others, in which latter process they need then not be destroyed or rebuilt. To represent a system with this type of dynamics as a complicated feedback automaton appears altogether appropriate. The abstract characteristics of this model have been dealt with at some length in the author's earlier book, and we refer readers who have a special interest to this and related works. Here it may suffice to say that the character of the organism as approximately a chemical feedback automaton has significant consequences with regard to its predictability. In the theory of automata this question appears under the guise of "reliability," a problem of obvious practical importance: What is the effect of an error made by the automaton at some step of its operation? Obviously, in a straight chain of causally connected events an error occurring at some moment will introduce errors in the events occurring thereafter. These later "errors" are not independent but are causal consequences of the earlier error, leading to a different information sequence from the one originally intended. If a system is sufficiently compartmentalized so that errors are prevented from spreading, their consequences may be limited to one compartment for a very long time. If this is not done the consequences of the error tend to spread over the whole system owing to the extensive interconnection of various processes by mutual feedback. Designers of electronic computers therefore have a pronounced tendency to compartmentalize their systems as much as possible, partly in order to prevent the spreading of errors and partly to be able to track them down more readily in case they occur. In the living cell there is little evidence of extreme compartmentalization, and the consequences of this state of affairs can readily be made clear.

Let us remember that according to quantum theory a measurement represents a perturbation of the system measured; in this sense it might be equated to an error committed by the component of the feedback system involved. Owing to the multiplicity of feedback couplings there will then be a tendency of the "error" to spread in time over the whole system. This amounts to saying that the inevitable perturbations which accompany any close determination of the molecular state of the specimen *cannot remain localized*, they must spread at a rate which of course depends on the rate of metabolism present. The consequences are not far to seek. Prediction of a system with numerous feedback couplings is likely to involve a much larger degree of indeterminacy in the long run than prediction of a system in which disturbances on the molecular scale remain comparatively localized (crystals being frequently systems of this type). To find out about the rate of spreading of errors or disturbances in a feedback system of considerable complexity would require an extensive and difficult mathematical analysis, which must be left to future theoreticians of biology. What we can state here is a qualitative result: In systems with multiple feedback couplings the deviations from the ordinary behavior caused by small-scale disturbances will, in the long run, be far more extensive and more widely distributed than similar disturbances would be in a system which is chemically less active and more homogeneous than a living cell.

Since we are speaking of automata and feedback cycles, let us try to be clear about one thing. An automaton is of course a system pertaining to physics pure and simple; it is usually governed by physical causality of a straightforward kind. It might also be built in such a way that certain of its variables change in a random fashion, in which case the output of the automaton will be a sort of mixture of causal and random processes.

1 · 15

The terms "physics," "physical," etc., do not have a very specific meaning in the context in which they have been used in the preceding sentences. They merely express a vague feeling arising from empirical evidence that there is a difference between non-living and living matter, but this difference ought to find expression in propositions of a theory. There is, however, no operational criterion which would tell us in unambiguous terms on the basis of some set of specified measurements that an object is or isn't alive. According to the views outlined above, the phenomenon of life cannot be described in terms of measurements on an individual object but *involves the relationship between the individual and an inhomogeneous class (or several such classes)*. The concept is somewhat difficult to grasp at first, as it deals with a realm of considerable abstraction. One thing is clear by definition: A class of objects may be considered to pertain to physics pure and simple if it is legitimate to analyze its behavior in terms of homogeneous classes. The degree of homogeneity need not be specified; it will suffice to assume that such inhomogeneity of the classes as is present is of no more than trivial significance. Just what is meant by this can be analyzed and decided only in special cases. In general terms, however, there can be no doubt about one rather decisive point: the theory of inhomogeneous classes is certainly not a special case of any theory of automata, nor, conversely, can automata by any stretch of the imagination be considered a special application of a theory of inhomogeneous classes. The two sets of concepts are logically independent. The discovery of automata theory has allowed the isolation of a number of processes which some investigators had considered characteristic of life and which have now been shown to be essentially properties of feedback systems. There is a widespread belief among biological as well as physical scientists that if traditional physics is extended by adding to it the theory of open systems and the theory of feedback systems (as well as so-called non-linear dynamics) most of the characteristic features of organisms can be analyzed and understood in terms of the physics and chemistry pertaining to this general systems concept. We need hardly point out again that these are in essence the *engineering* aspects of biology; they are

relevant to the highest degree, but they do not constitute the chief characteristic properties on which, according to the view presented here, a genuine biological
theory can be based; they are prerequisites.

A historical note is in order here. Driesch (a profound
and successful biological experimenter and thinker)
did not find acceptance when he tried to revive vitalism.
Thereafter, a number of distinguished biologists turned
to a less philosophically tinged approach. Disregarding
the ultimate relationship of the phenomena of life to
mechanical determinism, etc., these men tried to describe the most characteristic features of living organisms, as they are directly observed by modern methods,
on a *radically empirical* basis. This view is far removed
from any purely mechanistic biology; it brings out
clearly the strongly autonomous character of the behavior of organisms without, however, relating this character to any non-physical principles as the vitalists did.
This semi-theoretical approach has become known as
organismic biology. Although many outstanding biologists have contributed to this development, the author,
not wanting to go into particulars, wishes to single out,
more or less arbitrarily, a book by L. von Bertalanffy
(1952) as a specially clear and precise presentation of
this viewpoint.

There can be no doubt about the distinct advance
toward the unification of biology which has been
achieved by the organismic type of generalization. This
view puts strong emphasis on the character of organisms as open systems and also as feedback systems. If this
were all there is to organisms, this approach would be
just a mildly disguised form of mechanistic biology. Actually, *it is impossible to see*, from the work of von Bertalanffy for instance, whether or not this is all, and this fact
constitutes of course a remarkable weakness. We cannot

very well say that this failure lies just in the nature of the method, because similar positivistic approaches have been eminently successful in many problems of physical theory in the past and have indeed repeatedly led to philosophically profound consequences in theoretical physics (the point being that by a positivistically descriptive approach one is often able to eliminate implicit metaphysical assumptions). It must appear, in our case, that there is some specific, more or less hidden obstacle which makes this manner of approach less fruitful in biology than it is in physics. We believe this obstacle to lie in the tremendous variability, complexity, and inhomogeneity of organic matter. The critical step consists in taking these properties into account *explicitly*, as we have done in the principle of finite classes.

1 · 16

Let us now summarize the conditions which limit predictability in a complicated system:

(1) The randomness of molecular positions and velocities involved in kinetic theory (statistical mechanics).

(2) The unavoidable perturbations which, according to quantum mechanics, must occur as a result of measurements in the atomic and molecular domain. These are cumulative in composite systems.

(3) The presence of multiple feedback couplings, which results in a gradual spread of the perturbations mentioned under (2) over the whole system (e.g., cell).

(4) The limitations of knowledge resulting from the inapplicability of the method of sampling of homogeneous classes in systems of extreme complexity (principle of finite classes).

The reader will notice that conditions (1)–(3) are somewhat different in character from condition (4). The first three represent conditions existing in any physical system whatever, whether quite inhomogeneous or relatively homogeneous, assuming only that the system is composed of many molecules. Condition (4) on the other hand, while not mentioning biology explicitly, introduces radical inhomogeneity of *classes* and thereby singles out a significant type of abstraction. From there it will be much easier to penetrate toward a true theory of organisms.

1 · 17

In the preceding we have repeatedly spoken of an *open theory* as one in which many questions have no binary (yes-or-no) answers. From the positivistic viewpoint, the questions of most interest are those concerning prediction. The kind of openness so far considered described the pure randomness of individual events; it is the openness of probability theory. We then noted that in a system as extraordinarily complex as an organism, prediction may be far more limited than one would think at first sight. This brings us to the chief problem: Can there be a theory which is "more open" than the probabilistic ones, and what is the nature of this openness? We propose that there can be theories which contain *sets of regularities not all derivable from a common set of axioms*. This is only possible, of course, in a statistical universe of discourse where the statistical features, in a manner of speaking, buffer these regularities so that no mutual inconsistencies can appear. To be specific, then, we assume that there exist regularities in the realm of organisms whose existence cannot be logico-mathematically derived from the laws of physics, nor can a logico-mathematical contradiction be construed between these regularities and the laws of physics. In brief, the existence of such regularities can be neither proved nor disproved on the basis of the laws of physics. Questions regarding the derivation of these regularities from the laws of physics belong to the unanswerable kind.

Notice, however, that physics was defined as the science of homogeneous classes (classes that may be taken as of infinite membership). Our assumption can therefore be stated in more specific terms by saying that in *inhomogeneous classes of finite membership* there may exist regularities which have no equivalent in the corresponding homogeneous classes. To be more explicit, let us note again that we cannot know with exactitude the detailed molecular and electronic state of a system as comparatively large and complex as, say, a cell. We shall see in the next chapter that the number of available specific quantum states exceeds tremendously the number of cells that one could ever imagine to exist or to be at the disposal of even the most idealized observer. It is completely arbitrary to use the hypothesis (essentially of a metaphysical nature) that the object "is" in a definite molecular-electronic state. Moreover, there is only an altogether negligible chance that any two members of the inhomogeneous class "are" in comparable internal states.

Past vitalistic hypotheses always assumed that there is some non-physical principle which seizes upon matter and has a certain control of it while the object is alive. We do not here make any such claim, even though we assume the existence of regularities not deductively derivable from physics (homogeneous classes). We are only speaking of *properties of material objects,* the basic step forward having been made for us in quantum mechanics. There, we saw that owing to the fundamental importance of statistical features the laws of nature have to be formulated with respect to *classes*: we can say very little about an individual. We saw that the classes considered in physics are homogeneous classes, and the openness of the theory is of the probabilistic type. We then pass to inhomogeneous classes of finite membership and the openness of the theory now becomes of a more extensive type which we are calling here *organismic*; there are regularities in these classes which have no equivalent in the related homogeneous classes. Now in quantum mechanics it is fundamentally impossible to separate the theory into two parts, one representing rigorous orbits of mechanics and the other a superposed statistics (this was possible in the older theories on a "classical" basis). Similarly, it will be fundamentally impossible here to separate the regularities observed in inhomogeneous classes into a part pertaining to "physics" and a part pertaining to "biology." This is equivalent to the elimination of all dualistic features.

A theory of this type confronts us with two major problems:

(a) A formal proof must ultimately be furnished that generalized regularities of the type indicated are possible in suitable finite universes of discourse populated by inhomogeneous classes. If and when the present theory becomes accepted, this will undoubtedly constitute a major labor for mathematicians. This author has spent much effort in convincing himself that our reinterpretation of the widely used term "organismic" as representing regularities in inhomogeneous classes is both satisfactory on abstract grounds and promising on empirical biological grounds. Since the last-named, empirical relationships fill most of the remaining text, some of the more abstract and philosophical implications of our concepts will be sketched first.

(b) Not waiting for a formal proof of the type described to become available, one may introduce the *working hypothesis* that the chief characteristic of organisms is that they form classes which are radically inhomogeneous (where the number of members of any class is negligibly small compared to the number of internal states compatible with the characteristics of the class). Note that it is not the existence of inhomogeneous classes as such that forms the substance of the working hypothesis, this being mainly a matter of direct, observational experience; the nature of the working hypothesis is that *this is the most significant abstract property of organisms* and that it leads to observable regularities which have no direct equivalent in homogeneous classes. On the basis of this assumption we may try to achieve a conceptual reorganization of some of the empirical material, of what at present is called organismic biology; the test of the working hypothesis must of course be a much improved understanding of the theory, leading eventually to significantly new observational and experimental work.

1 · 18

One can give good reasons why, from an abstract viewpoint, it is necessary to have recourse to inhomogeneous classes. In the book already quoted, J. von Neumann gave a formal proof to the effect that quantum mechanics, in spite of its statistical features, is incompatible with the existence of regularities other than those which are deductively derivable from quantum theory itself. The nature of the proof can only be sketched here. Its basic tool is the concept of class averages (this concept need hardly be explained). Any kind of regularity, even a statistical one, gives rise to class averages of determinate values. It can be proved that in a homogeneous class of infinite membership, quantum mechanics determines all class averages *uniquely* and permits precise predictions of these averages for future times. Hence, any regularity which gives rise to predictable class averages must be such that these averages are identical with those given by quantum mechanics. One may infer from this by mathematical arguments that any regularity whatever must be derivable from quantum theory. If it were not so derivable, two sets of contradictory class averages could be constructed at the same time.

So far as one can see, there is no escape at all on mathematical grounds from the cogency of von Neumann's proof. Biology would then of necessity have to be purely mechanistic. As we need hardly say once more, the solution of the difficulty lies in the change of an *axiom*: the transition from infinite homogeneous classes to a finite universe of discourse populated by sufficiently inhomogeneous classes. Perhaps there are other ways of reconciling empirical biology with theoretical physics but the writer does not know of them, and he has found the approach propounded here singularly promising.

At first sight the existence of regularities in inhomogeneous classes looks somewhat like a self-contradictory proposition. This problem needs to be examined both from the wholly abstract, mathematical and from the conceptual, more philosophical viewpoint. The mathematical situation is as follows: The number of quantum states in which a member of the class may be is so vast that only a vanishingly small fraction of these states can ever be realized in any actual class. We cannot really know what state an individual member of the class is in, owing to the limitations of measurement discussed before. (To say that the object "is" in any specified state would be a purely metaphysical proposition.) As we have indicated, systems with multiple feedback couplings might differ in their development quite substantially in the long run, even though one may assume hypothetically that to begin with they are in states which are very close together. Only a vanishingly small number of the possible initial states are ever realized, so each such initial state represents *an extremely rare event*. In a homogeneous class of infinite membership any class average can be formed, but in a finite class, each of the members of which constitutes a very rare event, it is in general not possible to form all class averages. To appreciate this, let us consider the limiting case of an inhomogeneous class, namely, a class with one member only, a *one-class*, more commonly, an individual. In such a case, class averages are obviously meaningless. If the type of system considered is sufficiently complex, we are clearly not much better off if we have a class containing a hundred, or a million, specimens in place of one. In a crude way of speaking, the principle of finite classes comes down to this: the structural complexity and attendant class-inhomogeneity of organisms is always such that, no matter how large the actual number of specimens of the class (it might be billions of billions) the number of available internal states is invariably so much larger (it outruns the number of specimens as it were) that the set of actual specimens can be considered as a set of *exceedingly rare events* among all the possible events compatible with the characteristics of the class. This, then, is a formal prescription which, according to the view presented here, any theory of organisms must satisfy. But it is not a purely methodological device leading only to formal exercises; as a result of complexity and inhomogeneity there can, and there do in fact, in biological specimens, appear regularities within inhomogeneous classes, the existence of which could not be foreseen by a study of the properties of related homogeneous classes, however extensive this study might be.

Let us now look somewhat more closely at these regularities of inhomogeneous classes not derivable from homogeneous classes. What is the meaning of this concept? Imagine an idealized observer who has the capability of procuring a completely unlimited number of specimens of any class whatever. According to the formal arguments of von Neumann, such an observer can verify the laws of quantum mechanics, but nothing else. He will then find, however, that an utterly overwhelming fraction of his specimens, if followed over some length of time, are either simply dead or else are non-viable monstrosities. Only in extraordinarily rare instances will this observer find a specimen which behaves in a manner that we empirically designate as living. Now we assume of course that even the idealized observer cannot transcend the principles of quantum mechanics: he cannot find out in advance which specimens will turn out to be "alive" but can do so only *ex post facto*. This is so because if he wanted to go to great detail in finding out about the internal state of the object he would in any event have to kill it.

[The reader may notice a certain formal analogy between this type of argument and the plea for an abrogation of the second law of thermodynamics so often made by students of empirical biology. The latter step seems inadmissible to a physicist or statistician, since it would correspond to the modification of an axiom of statistical mechanics (randomness of molecular phases) far more fundamental than the axiom which we have modified (availability of infinite classes). The difficulty is abolished in the present theory because by the very nature of finite classes of the type considered here, any living structure is a tremendously rare event among all possible related structures.]

We should recall once more that quantum mechanics is a statistical science and that statistical prediction can be operationally verified *only* in terms of sufficiently large sets of samples. (The same is true of class averages, which are only an alternate way of expressing the existence of enough samples.) Predictability can be reduced in a statistical universe of discourse by limiting the available number of samples. At the same time, on making the available samples into representatives of exceedingly rare events, one denies the possibility that all observable regularities can be deduced as logico-mathematical consequences from the physical theory. For, in order to give this deduction an operational meaning, it would again be necessary to have a vastly larger set of samples than are ever available in actuality. Hence in sufficiently inhomogeneous, finite classes the existence of such non-deducible or partially non-deducible regularities need not lead to a logico-mathematical contradiction with physics.

We are now able to delineate more closely the character of these regularities not deductively derivable from physics which we take to be the essential feature of classes of organismic systems. Crudely speaking, an object looking outwardly like an organism can be healthy, sick, or dead. A healthy organism can sustain its physiological activity, its morphological features, and its reproductive ability. All this implies that the members of a class of organisms maintain a certain similarity of morphology and dynamics, both with themselves in time, and with other members of the class. The claim of the theory of finite classes is then that *not all of this similarity can be deductively derived by physics and chemistry from observable properties of the class.* Some of this can undoubtedly be explained in terms of the familiar stability of feedback automata together with the purely chemical stability of molecules; but in a class of organisms not all stability can be so derived. In other words, organismic behavior involves an *increased information stability,* both with respect to time in a single organism and with respect to the resemblance of the several members of the class. Part of this information stability can be explained mechanistically, part of it cannot, but the two are inextricably related; even to say "part-part" is a figure of speech without more than a very small fraction of operational meaning.

This theoretical approach conforms fully to the view expressed by Niels Bohr on the basis of quantum theory and expressed before him on general philosophical grounds by thinkers throughout the ages, that life is a *primary* phenomenon, not deducible from physics or anything else. Since, however, physics is valid in the organism, and since life according to the view proffered here can only appear through the inhomogeneity of structures and classes, the concept of the living state has a certain elusive quality which, in a more empirical context, has puzzled all the thinkers of biology. This elusiveness is, however, part of our most common experience. *No biological theory can possibly claim to be taken seriously unless it contains some symbolic representation of this elusiveness in its foundations.*

One should not think, however, that this makes biological theory void of operational content and incapable of verifiable prediction, etc. Merely, the theory is considerably more *open,* and its deductive organization far less stringent, then is the case in physics. One of the chief purposes of biological theory as conceived here is *to specify the limitations of physical prediction.* We mean by physical prediction in this context such prediction as is based on the laws of physics applied to models involving homogeneous classes. This type of investigation (into limitation of prediction) is a demanding task of great complexity, involving the detailed structural study of organic tissue, together with such statistical treatment of the inhomogeneity of classes as is required to describe the limitations of prediction quantitatively. We are dealing here assuredly with a set of operational procedures pertaining strictly to science and containing nothing, so far as we can see, that could be related to metaphysical speculations about life.

1 · 19

Beyond these negative aspects of organismic behavior there are of course positive, constructive ones, and these might best be approached by looking once more at certain typical differences in the behavior of organic as against inorganic matter. The nature of all physical law is such that it expresses a *differential relationship* with respect to time. If the state of a system at time t is given, the differential equations of physics permit us to compute the state of the system at a subsequent moment, $t + dt$. In classical physics this is true for the evolution in time of an individual object; in quantum mechanics, however, our statements are statistical; what changes as a function of time is a probability distribution. Physically, this corresponds to the statistical description of the behavior, in time, of a homogeneous class.

When feedback loops are involved matters become more complicated. Even then, if the system can be described "classically" (that is, if it can be followed from moment to moment by measurements which do not involve an appreciable perturbation of the object) the description of the system's evolution is in terms of differential equations which are not quite as simple as those prevailing in the absence of feedback; on the other hand they do not introduce any distinct features of a radically novel kind. Feedback alone is, however, not a sufficient criterion of organisms. There are, in addition, the several restrictions on the making of sufficiently thoroughgoing measurements which have been summarized in Section 1.16. The latter imply that any statistical uncertainty of prediction becomes vastly enhanced as time goes on. This notion of organismic behavior rests essentially on the impossibility of making sufficiently reliable predictions for systems of this kind.

By our definition, organismic systems exhibit regularities pertaining to inhomogeneous classes which cannot be fully deduced from those regularities that are quantitatively verifiable in the corresponding homogeneous classes. Since this argument depends critically on one's inability to resolve inhomogeneous classes into homogeneous classes, it becomes clear after a little reflection that behavior of the organismic type does not have the form of spatio-temporal continuous causality. Instead, speaking in a loose but we believe altogether intelligible way, we may say that organismic behavior expresses *integral relationships* of a kind that cannot be fully deduced from the differential relationships of physics. (The term "integral" is of course not used here in the rigorous sense of the mathematician but in the rather more general and slightly more vague sense in which an empirical biologist is wont to use it, in the sense of "biological integration.") Thus biology, insofar as it goes beyond the mere application of physics and chemistry, which latter remains of course fundamental, deals largely with the processes of integration, the term being now taken exactly in the meaning so familiar to the practicing biologist. But some of the logical vacuum which appears to surround the term "integration" if used only in a purely descriptive fashion disappears if we remember that such a statement has now a well-defined operational meaning: it refers to observable regularities in inhomogeneous classes.

From the vantage point we have reached it is possible to be once more rather specific about the formal distinction between physics and biology. Physics deals with *extensionality*. We are using this expression in place of "space-time" because it lends itself to a slightly broader meaning than the latter term. Thus we might subsume under it electromagnetic fields and the wave functions of quantum mechanics as representing space-time distributions. The abstract laws of physics, which deal with the quantitative relationships of extensionality, invariably take the form of differential equations in which the time is the independent variable.

The laws of biology on the other hand are expressed in terms of *class membership*. These classes, by definition composed of members showing similarity to each other, are inhomogeneous. The laws of biology express integral properties of dynamical systems; these systems, partly by virtue of common physical features, partly by their common integral properties, are analyzed in terms of their membership in more or less inhomogeneous classes. The class concept used here may to advantage be somewhat enlarged: An organism is a system of low physical predictability; that is, its behavior cannot be foreseen for long on the basis of the laws of physics as applied to measurements made on the system (measurements not sufficiently radical to disturb the organism severely). Hence morphological and physiological stability of an organism over more than very short periods constitutes essentially a property of the organismic type. This suggests that we may form *a class whose membership consists of one and the same organism* (in the sense of physical continuity) *taken at various points in time,* say minutes or hours apart, as the case may be. To repeat once more: biological theory deals with the regularities pertaining to class membership, whether the members of the class are distinct individuals or whether they represent the same individual at a succession of points in time.

The case of quantum mechanics and its prime application, theoretical chemistry, is intermediate, partaking of both forms of abstractions. On the one hand, the wave functions, being thought of as available in infinite sets, represent abstract constructs with space-time continuity and thus pertain to the realm of extensionality. On the other hand, the identity of all samples of physically equivalent systems in the same quantum state represents the simplest and most primitive example of a class, a precursor as it were of the far more complicated classes that appear in biology.

The reader will note that ours is not a unitary theory. So many current approaches to biological theory stress unitary aspects at the expense of thereupon becoming primitively mechanistic. Their critique will be implicit in the treatment of the consequences of our ideas given in the third chapter. In the unitary theories the essential implications of the radical inhomogeneity of classes is ignored, "smeared out" as it were, the corresponding objects being treated as if they formed homogeneous classes equivalent to those commonly found in the experiments of the physicist and chemist. In the theory proposed here we intend to achieve a closer approach to the properties of organisms by introducing a new formal element, the analysis of the properties of radically inhomogeneous classes.

1 · 20

The distinction between extensionality on the one hand and class properties on the other leads us into a somewhat marginal question, namely, the role which mathematics may have to play in theoretical biology as against its function in theoretical physics. Geometry, calculus, and related forms of mathematics are the tools for dealing with extensionality. It is therefore only natural that these branches of mathematics should have grown up inextricably interrelated with the growth of physics throughout the history of both sciences.

The concept of a finite universe of discourse populated by inhomogeneous classes is a purely abstract one; it satisfies the most severe criteria one could establish, from an extreme positivistic viewpoint, for the exclusively relational and non-metaphysical character of theory construction. Nevertheless, its formal structure is quite different from that of any scheme of pure extensionality. The very nature of class inhomogeneity precludes to some extent that uniformity and mathematical rigor to which the theoretical physicist is accustomed. Mathematics, as Willard Gibbs said, is a language; mathematical analysis is the language *par excellence* wherewith to describe extensional relationships. Abstract relationships of classes, inclusion, exclusion, overlap, etc., can be represented in terms of the symbolism of formal logic. Probabilistic statements, again, can be expressed by conventional mathematical formalism. But of course in all these cases the representation becomes the more involved the more complex the relationships to be described.

One should not forget, therefore, that ordinary conceptual language has clearly been invented for biological purposes. Basic concepts are patterned after the classes of biology, be they trees, cows, or cockroaches. If complexity reaches a certain degree, the common language of everyday intercourse may be more enlightening than a thicket of mathematical formulas. In fact, the more one relies on common mathematical formalism in theory formation, the more one is likely to bring out, and perhaps to overestimate, those properties of organized systems which represent extensionality at the expense of those which correspond to class inhomogeneity and which therefore tend to be more intimately related to organismic behavior.

This is not a plea for or against mathematical formalism as compared to ordinary conceptual language. But a warning might be in place against confusing the use of mathematical formalism with theory. If relationships become too complex, conceptual expression may well be the most appropriate way of formulating certain aspects of theory, and, given the inhomogeneity of many classes of biology, conceptual language may frequently be the more suitable and appropriate means of expressing the basic relationships pertaining to the regularities of biological theory. Since, however, the relationships of extensionality are as fundamental in the world of organisms as they are everywhere in the physical world, it is likely that in practice the two languages will complement each other instead of one of them gradually replacing and expelling the other, as it might appear to those sometimes overly given to mechanistic modes of thought.

Again, in this context we should not overlook an aspect of the theoretical approach presented in this work that has been implicitly alluded to before and that is intimately related to the choice of language. We have in mind that the method of progression from the well-established relationships of extensionality which physics has uncovered into the realm of class properties, especially those of inhomogeneous classes which are at the basis of biology, ought to be a *gradual* one. This corresponds to a gradual progression from the closed extensional scheme of theory represented by classical physics to the more and more *open* forms of theory which are required in biology. The feeling of a certain flatness which seems to be the invariable accompaniment of purely mechanistic theories is not present here, owing largely to the fact that the increase in complexity as expressed through the device of inhomogeneous classes is an *autonomous* phenomenon rather than a mere piling up of more and more complicated machinery. As a result, we find ourselves closer to traditional philosophical concepts than some other attempts at biological theorizing have been. We are inclined to consider this an advantage of this type of approach. We are equally far removed from a pat mechanism as we are from an intrinsically dualistic vitalism.

1 · 21

Before we apply the preceding general ideas to more concrete biological data it might be beneficial to test them against a summary view of the general, conceptual side of present-day biological science. We are here in a most fortunate position. Some ten years ago the Biology Council of the U.S. National Academy of Sciences, under the chairmanship of Professor Paul Weiss, organized an informal symposium among a dozen leading American biologists drawn from a variety of branches of the life sciences. The meeting took place in the fall of 1955, lasting for three days of almost continuous discussion. Its chairman, Professor Ralph W. Gerard later edited and published a lengthy transcript of the proceedings (1958). The title, "Concepts of Biology," sufficiently characterizes the aim and compass of the endeavor. We are particularly indebted to Professor Weiss for drawing our attention to this publication after the appearance of the author's earlier book, and for pointing out the similarities of some ideas with those sketched by us. The quotations given below are literal (with occasional condensations) and frequently reflect the informal and colloquial character of the discussion which has been retained in the transcript by its editor.

We begin by noting a rather ambitious undertaking, a definition of life by R. D. Hotchkiss (p. 129): *"Life is the repetitive production of ordered heterogeneity."* It appears from reading the body of the transcript and from the repetition of this statement in the summary by R. W. Gerard at the end, that this definition met with the approval of the biologists present. Notice now, the importance of "heterogeneity." If this term were omitted, the statement would collapse into the almost trivial proposition that nature has laws. We need hardly point out the intimate similarity of this statement to the nature of the formal approach to theoretical biology described in the preceding pages. The reader may here judge for himself.

The notion of ordered heterogeneity leads one naturally into questions about the character of the order which exists beyond, and seemingly in spite of, heterogeneity. F. O. Schmitt expresses himself as follows (p. 144): "We have in the macromolecular complexes of cells and tissues and their components a type of ordering which is unique to those cells and tissues. And this is produced by the living organism upon substrates which themselves have no ordering or, if they have, this ordering has been reduced first, and then the reordering impressed on it. . . . Inherent in this is not only the reduction of the original ordered parts to more disordered parts and the eventual production of a new type of order, but also the interaction mechanism wherein energy is provided at specific loci in order to produce the new ordering. It is not sufficient for a helix of DNA, RNA, or protein to have some molecule come to lie across it, as some information theorists seem to think, and bingo, you've synthesized a new molecule! It takes a whole series of intermediary steps of biosynthesis before that can be accomplished, and here I think you have the essence of some of the 'living' aspects of organisms, namely this beautiful organization, in time and space, of the energy-giving reactions with what might be called the ordering reaction. I will coin the phrase: ordered coupling of energy."

The present author may be permitted some comments on this statement. What we find described here is of course exactly what we would call an organismic process or, in our current terminology, the transformation of microscopic inhomogeneity into ordered extensionality. Nobody would want to doubt the basic role of multiple chemical feedback couplings in these processes. Their overall orderliness is here amply emphasized. Our question is whether all of this observed regularity can be derived logico-mathematically from the laws of physics (as stated in terms of homogeneous classes), and our answer is that it is only in part so derivable; a large fraction of the order is organismic, that is, partly *autonomous*, the processes being intrinsically impredictable from a knowledge of the theory of homogeneous classes, owing to the fundamental limitations of measurement and prediction discussed before. We see also clearly that lack of physical predictability does not mean lack of order and regularity; it means the failure of "reductionism," that is, of the doctrine that all organismic order can ultimately be derived logically from the properties of molecules. But let us return to our symposium report.

We find P. Weiss making the following statement

(p. 140): "Well, I'll try to stay out of philosophy and be strictly operational. First, 'life is a complex of phenomena and is a process, therefore the unit of life can never be a particle or static body, but has to be a unitary elementary *process*'. . . . The total process has a greater degree of invariance than the individual component parts. . . . As we proceed from the parts to the collective, the collective shows greater stability or invariance. If this is true, then it immediately leads to the postulate of a hierarchy of levels. But this constancy or invariance is true not only at one level, a molecule or a molecular assembly, but repeats itself at the level of the cell component, of the cell, of the tissue, of the organism, and so on.

"This immediately leads to the next consideration; if there is this relative invariance at the collective level, there must be an interrelation, obviously, of the individual constituents. The parts are non-identical, diverse, that is what we call heterogeneity of composition. But the thing that is constant is not the composition as such, but the order of that heterogeneity; in time, it's the orderly sequence; in space, it's the orderly arrangement. . . . If the individual parts are interrelated in their reactions, they then establish ecological systems that are mutually helpful to each other, or at least compatible. If this is true on the level of society, organisms in groups, cells in tissues, then the same thing can be said of the elementary biochemical reactions within the cell. Therefore, I coined the term 'molecular ecology' which is distinct from the biochemistry of an homogenate. Molecular ecology means that individual reactions are interrelated in such a way that what one does is an existential requirement for its neighbors, and *vice versa*.

"This next leads to the introduction of statistics and an assertion of the non-identity of any living systems.

The idea of the identity of cells—any two cells, any two individuals, and so on—is a fiction. The problem of individuality is merely an expression of the fact that you do have this greater constancy at the higher level of the organized individual system than you have of its constituent parts. That is, identical twins are much more similar than are any microscopic sections from corresponding sites you can lay through either of them."

The principle of the dissimilarity of individuals seems to be generally shared by the participants of this conference. Thus Ernst Mayr (p. 132) : "Another difference [between the living and non-living] is the problem of individuality, such that no two individuals, no two species, are the same. Such complete individuality is, on the whole, absent from the physical world, which often makes it very difficult when a physicist and a biologist get together. The physicist, unfamiliar with this type of thing, has great difficulty in understanding it." A little later we hear D. R. Goddard (p. 135) : "I think that methodologically, operationally, this [individuality] is a very important aspect of biology. True, we do have populations that may be worked with and they may be unique —a bacteriologist may deal with and study the properties of the culture as a whole. But, by and large, most biologists are operating with individuals and, what's more, these individuals are not identical. Usually they will be so uniform that we define them by certain terms, but we must recognize that each is separate. We also study individual responses or processes of the single organism. . . . I think this is an important aspect of our science operationally; whether or not it's going to make a great deal of difference in our conceptual framework might be debated." A little later, E. W. Caspari agrees (p. 137): "No individual is ever identical with any other individual." Finally, to bring out once more the role of individuality as a significant factor above and beyond the mere configurational variability of physical systems, we quote a comment by R. W. Gerard (p. 143) : "I want to put [variability] at a level that may be more meaningful. Individuality may be extremely important, but not because the molecules are in different states."

The issue is then clearly stated in the comment just quoted, by D. R. Goddard, that it is open to debate whether inhomogeneity and individuality play a fundamental role in the conceptual framework of theoretical biology. While the ultimate answer to this question may be in the distant future, the elaboration of all aspects of the working hypothesis that it does play such a role need not be postponed.

CHAPTER 2 · STATISTICS AND THE CONCEPT OF IMMENSITY

2·1

In biology there is often a certain looseness in the definition of the objects dealt with; this looseness springs, in part at least, from the fact that a living and a dead system cannot be told apart in terms of a purely static picture. Life requires metabolism or, more generally, the dynamics of transformations. We can, however, think in an abstract way of the picture of a biological system at a given instant of time. We shall designate such an instantaneous picture as a *system event*. The life process is then schematized as a series of transformations between system events. We need not now specify the amount of observational knowledge that goes into the characterization of a system event. This amount is limited by virtue of the arguments which were enumerated in Section 1.16. Here, we shall not ask what becomes of the system later nor shall we denote any special type of observation. It will suffice to say that what we mean by a system event is essentially a three-dimensional, purely spatial picture of the organism based on whatever data we choose to include; in the language of the physicist a system event is a three-dimensional "cut," at a given instant, through the four-dimensional space-time manifold.

It is now convenient (although of course by no means indispensable) to define the classes that we use in biological theory in such a way that the members of any class are system events. Classes so defined represent morphology (static aspects) whereas transformations of systems events pertain to physiology (dynamic aspects).

Next, in what follows the terms *macro* and *micro* will be used in the context of atomic and molecular physics rather than in their biological meaning, the latter of which is closer to everyday usage. A system will be designated as microscopic when its known details are on the atomic scale, geometrically or energetically, that is, if the description includes, say, individual wave functions of electrons, etc. If on the other hand the description is restricted to a level well above that where individual atomic details, in particular quantum effects, make their appearance we designate it as macroscopic. Correspondingly, we shall designate as *macrovariable* any quantity whose measurement does not significantly involve quantum effects. This implies that a macrovariable can be measured without having the measurement produce an appreciable perturbation of the object. It is therefore possible to measure a macrovariable repeatedly with consistent results, and it may well be admissible to measure it by several very different methods. (We must not, however, be too demanding in requiring extreme accuracy, otherwise destructive perturbations again become inevitable.) We recall once more from Chapter 1 that the concept of a macrovariable is not capable of rigorous delimitation: there is an essentially *gradual* transition to the variables of the microscopic realm, and this gradualism must in our view be present in any scheme of theoretical biology.

2·2

Certain characteristics of living tissue are determined at the expense of destroying it. This is particularly true of structural properties of complex chemical constituents. As a rule the investigator needs to grind up enough material so that he can make chemical determinations *in vitro*. Such quantities, descriptive of the organism under study, will be designated as its *homogeneous compo-nents*. They are characterized by the fact that their exist-ence in the system considered can be inferred from (usu-ally disruptive) measurements on other members of the class.

At the other end of the scale there is the notion of a microscopic state fully determined in all its details to within the limitations set by quantum mechanics. Ideal-ly, this corresponds to a description of the state of the entire system in terms of a single wave function of quan-tum theory. Such a state of maximum knowledge is in biology an idealization, although according to the no-tions of quantum mechanics an entirely legitimate one. It will be designated as a *microstate*. Since in practice the determination of a specific microstate (single wave func-tion) for an organism would be effectively meaningless owing to the destructive character of the corresponding measurements, there will be many microstates represent-ing the same macroscopic system; the microstates can only be considered *probabilistically*. It now seems a rea-sonable assumption that, inasmuch as we do not wish to make destructive measurements, an organism can only be described by means of a sufficient number of macro-variables and homogeneous components, leaving the microstates to statistics.

Now the most conspicuous fact about the microstates is their extraordinarily large number. This is familiar to any student of statistical mechanics. We shall illus-trate it by an example. Consider a polar molecule in aqueous solution which can dissociate into a pair of ions. Although the molecules are indistinguishable with re-spect to their properties, they can be distinguished in the solution in terms of the coordinates of each molecule or ion. Let there be n molecules of which n_1 are dissociated so that n_1/n is the degree of dissociation. To avoid singular cases, let n_1/n be neither very small nor very close to unity. Simple calculations given in every textbook of statistical mechanics show that the number N of micro-states (that is, the number of ways in which the disso-ciation can be "partitioned" among the n molecules) can be expressed by the approximate formula

$\log N = n \log n - n_1 \log n_1 - (n - n_1) \log (n - n_1)$

It does not matter how we choose the base of the log-arithm, so for simplicity let us choose logarithms to the base ten. Now the second and third term on the right-hand side of this equation are clearly smaller than the first term; thus we have in a crude but for us sufficient approximation

$$N = 10^{n \log n}$$

If we take for n ten billion, which is certainly a small number as molecules go, we see that

$$N = 10^{100,000,000,000}$$

Numbers of this magnitude appear commonly in statisti-cal mechanics; they are characteristic of that particular science. We shall introduce a terminology convenient for the purpose: a number whose logarithm is itself a large number will be designated as *immense*. If the ratio of two numbers, a/b, is an immense quantity, we shall say that a is immensely large compared to b, or conversely that b is immensely small compared to a. Note here that we have not defined an immense number in absolute terms; we have expressed the definition of an immense number in terms of a decision as to when another num-ber (its logarithm) is considered "large." The decision as to when a given number is to be designated as large is purely a matter of convention; hence the same holds for the term "immense."

Immense numbers are obtained whenever we determine the number of microstates (the number of possible "partitions") which satisfy a given set of thermodynamical and chemical conditions. Systems in the chemist's laboratory are as a rule highly homogeneous. For the radically inhomogeneous systems of biology, conditions are not so simple, but the general result can be applied there also: *The characterization of a system event by macrovariables and homogeneous components is compatible in each case with an immense number of microstates.*

2 · 3

There is of course a science that deals specifically with the way in which systems, or more precisely classes, can be described in terms of a limited number of macrovariables, the latter being obtained by forming averages over an immense number of microstates. This is statistical mechanics. For the sake of brevity the term "kinetics" will sometimes be used in a strictly synonymous sense. We ought to emphasize, however, that we are not just dealing with thermodynamical equilibria, as is often the case in applications of statistical mechanics. It is quite true of course that in the past statistical mechanics was more often than not restricted to thermodynamical equilibria, that is, systems which, macroscopically considered, are static or at the least quasi-static, in cases where transformations are involved. The systematic exploration of non-equilibrium kinetics, which has been so vigorously pursued in more recent years, has brought to light a vast variety of phenomena and has illuminated the complexity appearing in kinetic processes even for very modest deviations from equilibrium. Going much farther in the same direction we find that the measurability of a living organism, whenever we want to keep it alive and intact, is severely limited by the principles summarized in Section 1.16. There is no doubt that if these limitations are observed, the number of microstates among which a choice can be made, but which cannot be individually distinguished by experiment, is immense. Since the science of representations involving immense numbers of microstates is statistical mechanics it follows that from our viewpoint any theory of organisms implies the application of a general form of statistical mechanics to radically inhomogeneous systems and classes. This apparently innocent statement has many weighty consequences; in particular it restricts theories of organisms to those which are expressible in terms of certain models of statistical mechanics.

When statistical mechanics is applied to equilibria or near-equilibria of homogeneous systems there are usually only a few significant macroscopic variables, for instance, temperature, specific volume, and relative concentrations of various reaction partners. One assumes as a matter of course that the details of the immense number of microstates compatible with the macrovariables are irrelevant; *they average out*. Equilibria as well as gradual changes of equilibria corresponding to certain chemical reaction rates can then be calculated, given enough knowledge of molecular structure. Now we remember that we decided to represent a living organism in a schematical manner as a sequence of system events, that is, cuts across the spacetime manifold at certain instants separated by suitably chosen intervals of time. The distinction between mechanistic and non-mechanistic biology can now be quite clearly exhibited. The hypothesis that system events can always be adequately predicted from previous system events, using nothing but the laws of physics, constitutes the mechanistic or reductionist hypothesis. Note that by our previous definition a system event contains, by way of its macrovariables, information indicative of previous states of the individual and also contains in its homogeneous components information pertaining to the class (or classes.)

The use of statistical mechanics implies that immense numbers of microstates are indistinguishable from each other on the basis of the permissible measurements. We know from experience that in homogeneous systems and classes these microstates can be averaged out, leaving us with only a limited number of well-defined macrovariables. The question to be raised is whether this averaging process can be carried out successfully in the radically inhomogeneous systems and classes of biology. If we assume that this is not always so, as we do in the type of theory advanced here, then we also imply that prediction of system events cannot always be carried out to an adequate degree—by adequate we mean here that in comparison with later observations we are not losing too much by disregarding more or less irrelevant individual variations. Now if the regularities which we are able to find in the classes of biology are not simply consequences of physics in a reductionist fashion, then we have almost tautologically two kinds of prediction. The first kind makes use solely of the laws of physics to extrapolate given sets of observations to the future; it could be carried out by an observer who knows physics and has perfect measuring and computing equipment but who might never have studied organisms at all (if such an idealization be permitted). We shall call these *physical predictions*. The second kind of prediction is based directly on the empirical properties of organisms (for instance the fact that an acorn under favorable conditions germinates and grows into an oak tree). The writer has learned from lengthy experience that the distinction between these two types of prediction is somewhat difficult to grasp for those who have not had extensive experience with the abstractions of theoretical physics. To understand the concept of a physical prediction we need to remember that prediction as practiced by physicists and chemists invariably requires the (perhaps implicit) assumption that the sample of observations (necessarily finite in practice) upon which the prediction is based can be embedded in a homogeneous class of infinite membership—and the prediction really refers to this class. Another implicit assumption is that whatever quantities are not uniform in the homogeneous class are effectively random. According to the viewpoint here presented any deviations from mechanistic (reductionist) philosophy imply that the scheme of infinite homogeneous classes is to be abandoned in favor of a description employing finite, radically inhomogeneous classes. Hence these two types of predictions contain no more nor less than what we had expressed in the first chapter as the distinction between the two different types of universes of discourse. It expresses it in alternate, sometimes more convenient language. Physical prediction is that type of prediction which implicitly assumes infinite homogeneous classes; whether more general types of prediction are possible in biology cannot be rashly prejudged. The degree of predictability, of course, depends on the degree of measurability of the details of the system or class considered.

Now in dealing with statistical mechanics we are in general forced to an extensive renunciation of knowledge to a degree which vastly exceeds the limitations imposed upon the measurement of a single elementary particle. This is always true if we are concerned with the time-dependence of a macroscopic object, and it applies particularly to organisms, since they are objects of the highest complexity. The appearance of statistical mechanics in this context is thus fundamental. Physics and chemistry have developed certain basic concepts relating to atoms and molecules; in terms of these concepts the fundamental experiments of atomic physics as well as observations on *homogeneous* classes can be successfully interpreted. The science concerned with the construction of models for inhomogeneous bodies or classes must be a generalized form of statistical mechanics. In any kinetic model an immense number of microstates remain undetermined so that only statistical statements about them can be made. We therefore claim that in such a theory whatever *autonomy* (more precisely, semi-autonomy) *can exist for classes of organisms flows from our unavoidable ignorance regarding immense numbers of microstates*; this ignorance leaves us with a lack of physical predictability of future system events. This approach to theoretical biology is purely relational, conforming to the positivistic viewpoint; it has to do with the building up of *models*, having given macrovariables, out of an immense number of microstates about which only statistical statements can be made.

2 · 4

To repeat once more, the concept of autonomous or, rather, semi-autonomous biology makes sense to us only if it says precisely this: There are observable regularities in biological classes which are intrinsically impossible to deduce in their entirety logico-mathematically from the laws of physics. (One may assume the latter as known, without need to enter here into philosophical discussions on that point.) We now ought to make sure that this notion of semi-autonomy is free from internal contradictions. This is particularly necessary since the whole concept clearly contradicts von Neumann's proof, quoted in Chapter 1, to the effect that the validity of quantum mechanics is not compatible with the existence of any other type of regularity in nature which would not be derivable from quantum theory itself. We have shown how this proof becomes invalidated if one goes from a universe of discourse composed of homogeneous classes of infinite membership to a finite universe of discourse in which radically inhomogeneous classes exist. We may break up the conditions for the lack of adequate prediction into two parts:

(1) Since we propose to operate within a finite universe of discourse, we may assume that if we hypothetically assign to any system event occurring in reality one specific microstate, then the number of microstates of any class in this universe will be negligible compared to the number of microstates which are theoretically possible: any actual microstate is as a rule an immensely rare event among all possible ones. This condition implies that the formation of *all* possible class averages (inclusive of averages over all microvariables, since a complete set of averages is a prerequisite for von Neumann's proof) becomes devoid of operational meaning for some of these averages.

(2) The variability of microstates must not average out as they do in homogeneous systems and classes. Instead, this variability must modify a cascade of feedback cycles, ultimately influencing the macrovariables. If the macrovariables show regularities, as of course they do, then we may be able to use these to infer the properties of the particular microstates which are required to generate these macrovariables. If, however, the members of the class are radically inhomogeneous at all levels of their organization, this "retrodiction" may be unsuccess-

ful in the sense that a large number of microstates, each having characteristics rather different from any other, can be equally compatible with the given macrovariables. Since on the other hand the experimental determination of a microstate so far as it can be achieved is radically destructive, this very limited retrodiction does not help us sufficiently to allow prediction of macrovariables for other members of the class. We shall presently return to this cardinal point of biological dynamics: the interaction of variables at various levels of size and organization.

2·5

The abstract properties just discussed are in the nature of necessary postulates indicating the nature of a non-mechanistic biological scheme which does not contradict physics. We can go one step further and show that they conform in a rather general way to certain empirical circumstances. First, somewhat surprisingly, taking a cue from the astronomers, we can obtain an order-of-magnitude idea of the size of the actual universe and use this to determine an upper bound on the *number of system events* which may sensibly be assumed in any hypothetical finite universe of discourse. This was first done in the author's earlier book (1958, p. 159), and the train of thought will be briefly reproduced. We take a single cell as a representative organism. We assume that there can be no more than 10^9 cells per cm^2 of the earth's surface at any one time. We next fix the interval between system events. This was earlier taken as one minute, but one millisecond, or even one microsecond would do as well. This gives us the total number of system events that can occur on the planet during the lifetime of the universe, the latter taken, by way of an upper limit, as 3.10^{10} years. Astronomers estimate that there are some 10^{20} planets in the universe—to within quite a few powers of ten of course. Putting all this together we find that the number of system events of any class of cells in the real universe should not exceed 10^{70}. It is undoubtedly true that this number is *immensely small,* in the exact sense defined before, compared to the number of microstates that are compatible with the ascertainable macrovariables of any class of cells.

The reader has every right to frown on this speculative juggling of big numbers against a background of cosmology. There are, however, two good reasons for going through such an argument at least once before proceeding further. One of these reasons is that the homogeneity of the classes of atomic physics prevails even on a cosmic scale: we have every reason to believe that a hydrogen atom on the Andromeda nebula is indistinguishable from a hydrogen atom in our laboratory. This fact, by no means trivial, forces anybody who deals with finite classes as a tool of description to have at least a cursory glance at the cosmological implications of the class concept employed, if only to protect himself from crushing criticism of this abstraction. Having once looked at such speculative implications, one may then ignore them and go back to use the concept of finite classes just as a matter of methodology.

The second reason why this slight exercise in cosmological numbers is of some use is that it affords an antidote against the kind of reasoning derived from Newtonian mechanics and commonly attributed to Laplace (it is very widespread, however, and Laplace himself was no doubt intensely aware of its speculative character) ; this is the notion that in the microscopic realm there are atoms or molecules which have definite positions and motions in space after the manner of the planets in the solar system. While the advent of quantum theory has forced us to revise these notions and to use a different analytical and conceptual approach to microscopic observations, there has often been a tendency to employ wave functions merely as a substitute for the older billiard-ball models; this habit, if applied to biology, leads readily to reductionist modes of thought. What we are trying to show here is that the use of physical theory must be restricted much further, namely to *kinetic models* of radically inhomogeneous systems and classes. In such models *there exists no unique relationship between the observable macrovariables and any one specific microstate*. What the "cosmological" arguments of the preceding paragraphs indicate is that this indeterminacy is not caused by the limitation of our mental horizon to some specific segment of the world.

2 · 6

Having discussed the first of the two conditions set down above—the condition which says that an actual microstate, although unknown, is statistically speaking an immensely rare event among possible microstates—we take up the second condition. This condition says, roughly speaking, that the variability of microstates must be coupled, through a suitable cascade of feedback cycles, into the dynamics of the macrovariables, which thereby lose part of their physical predictability. The assumption that a coupling of this type exists is at present no more than an hypothesis. It is the one hypothesis of a physical nature that we require; all the other propositions so far introduced are, if closely scrutinized, either methodological devices or formalizations of thoroughly established empirical facts.

That organisms show structure as well as inhomogeneities of this structure at any level has been known for a long time. But before the advent of the electron microscope the region between the dimensions of microns, capable of resolution by the ordinary microscope, and the dimensions of angstroms, the realm of atoms and molecules, remained relatively unexplored. This comprises a factor of 10^4 in linear dimensions. Electron microscopy has shown that in organic tissue there exist structures of various kinds at *all* levels down to the atomic one, and also inhomogeneities corresponding to these structures (see for instance Frey-Wyssling, 1953, for a somewhat older but very elegant review). One cannot doubt that there are also physico-chemical processes whose magnitude corresponds to these levels, and these processes almost certainly involve all kinds of feedback couplings. Therefore, the idea that there are dynamical couplings all the way up and down between the macrovariables and the microstates is in a qualitative way in excellent agreement with the empirical evidence. If the hypothesis holds, then, as the organism metabolizes, the inhomogeneity of the microstates will gradually "feed" into the macrovariables and will result in a partial impredictability of the latter.

It is hard to overestimate the importance which the peculiar dynamics of the organism as just sketched must have for the character of biological theory. In the statistical mechanics of the conventional, homogeneous inorganic systems we have as a rule a very clear distinction between macrovariables and microvariables. Take the classical case of a gas: here the macrovariables such as pressure, temperature, specific heat, viscosity, and others can be measured with great precision. But then, as we go to smaller and smaller dimensions we find essentially nothing new beyond random variability until we come to the molecules or atoms themselves. There we find masses and structural properties of atoms and molecules which are stable features and can be ascertained with extraordinary precision. Thus we have two levels, a "lower," molecular one and an "upper," macroscopic one, which are related in a statistical manner: the macrovariables are averages over properties pertaining to very many molecules; the sharpness and stability of the macrovariables is a direct result of the large numbers of molecules involved in the formation of these averages.

Sometimes one obtains a better approximation by distinguishing three levels in place of two. This applies particularly to crystalline solids where there is a level (or perhaps a spectrum of levels) encompassing crystal defects, dislocations, and, on a somewhat larger scale, crystal grains whose size and the corresponding energetic magnitudes are often intermediate between those of molecules and those of the fully macroscopic variables. It may then happen that individually ascertainable properties of the intermediate scale have a specific influence on properties of a much larger scale: a typical example is the breaking of a solid rod as the result of a localized minute flaw in its texture, which under stress expands into a crack.

Somewhat more involved interactions between levels corresponding to different geometrical sizes are found in the dynamics of fluids, especially when turbulence occurs. Under certain conditions instabilities of flow are latent in the fluid but require the action of a minor local disturbance to take effect, whereupon a large eddy may develop. It is usually almost impossible to predict the exact time and place this will happen. Also it is a common feature of turbulent flow that larger eddies give rise to the appearance of smaller eddies, again owing to intrinsic instabilities of the motion. Here we have, in a very crude manner of speaking, a higher level of organization influencing a lower level. In some respects such hydrodynamical phenomena, as well as the mechanical ones like breakage, are particularly interesting because they take place purely in the realm of "classical" physics, almost invariably altogether beyond the level at which quantum phenomena play any role.

If we compare these somewhat randomly culled examples illustrative of inorganic systems with the dynamics of organisms the difference becomes rather clear. In the inorganic systems, the effects of phenomena at one size or level upon another level, whenever they are not simply and straightforwardly the result of averaging processes, are rather haphazard and incidental. In the organism, on the other hand, the couplings among various levels of organization appear *systematized*; they exist everywhere and always as long as metabolism takes place. Even though the very large body of existing observations might in the future be still more extended, it is already clear that feedback loops almost certainly exist in the connections of *all* levels. We admire here the perspicuity of Leibniz (see Section 1.7), who long before the advent of modern biology came so close to recognizing this basic characteristic of organisms. Our only quarrel with Leibniz will be that these couplings do not, as he thought, continue down to infinitely small parts, but stop at the atomic level. Beyond all this, we cannot help thinking that in the course of the original appearance of life on earth there was a gradual evolution from a very primitive type of organization with correspondingly simple couplings to types containing more and more complex couplings. But it must seem altogether probable that the intermediate forms of organization, which would at the same time exhibit less fully developed kinds of dynamical couplings between levels, have been superseded by the biologically better adapted, highly complex ones which we now observe. The lower forms with the less highly developed dynamical couplings are therefore likely to have long since disappeared.

These comments may help to bring out more clearly a formal point: There is a difference in the application of our basic method—that of description in terms of finite, radically inhomogeneous classes—as between the inorganic and the organic case; for inorganic systems it is just exactly as true as for organisms that in a finite world the number of objects of not too minute a size (say for instance of sand or dust grains) is immensely small compared to the number of microstates in terms of which these objects can be represented by kinetic models, but this fact is for all practical purposes *irrelevant*, it has no dynamical consequences. In organisms on the other hand the couplings between levels of organization, reaching all the way up and down, constitute an indispensable tool of the organism. They permit the radical inhomogeneity of any class in the realm of the microvariables to give rise to macroscopic effects whose physical prediction becomes at least partially impossible owing to the presence of these very couplings. Thus the existence of these dynamical couplings constitutes the *necessary precondition* for the extensive lack of physical predictability in organisms.

2 · 7

By way of comparison with our preceding ideas we may mention here an interesting approach to biological theory, perhaps best designated as semi-mechanistic, by the German physicist P. Jordan (1948), who was also one of the founders of quantum theory. Jordan proposes an "amplifier theory" of organisms. He thinks that the organism may be equipped with amplifying devices which transform purely statistical features of microphysics into macroscopic actions, thus introducing a lack of predictability which is not present in ordinary macroscopic mechanisms. While we may feel a certain sympathy with Jordan's approach, we can direct two criticisms against his ideas. In our present scheme, the ultimate processes that lead to a failure of physical prediction and hence to the notion of organismic regularities may well be considered as representing a form of amplification, but the corresponding individual processes are *not strictly localizable*. The behavior of the regularities is related to our ignorance of immense numbers of microstates in the kinetic models employed. It seems to us that our model is here more realistic than Jordan's with respect to the limits of measurability in the tremendously complex realm of organic structures.

Secondly and mainly, however, as the analysis of Chapter 1 has shown, any biological theory remains a mere specialization of quantum mechanics so long as the construction of classes of unlimited membership is a permissible idealization. Whenever class membership is sufficiently large (immense) all averages, even those of microphysics, are uniquely determined. It then follows from von Neumann's theory that all regularities in the class are deducible from the regularities of atomic physics. This shows once more that the introduction of individually unpredictable but statistically fully determinate features, which is the essence of Jordan's ideas, does not form an adequate basis for autonomous biology; the use of a finite universe of discourse is an essential prerequisite.

2 · 8

The reader may long since have noticed that the arguments of this chapter are related to certain aspects of traditional philosophy, in particular that branch of it which is known as epistemology, the theory of knowledge. How much can we know about the detailed structure of an object? Clearly, one need not be a philosopher to realize that this is a basic question when one deals with the predictability of objects as complex and intricate as organisms. Therefore, it might be useful to re-examine some of the notions just discussed in such a way that their epistemological implications are more clearly recognizable.

Epistemology like any other intellectual activity has grown historically from a less differentiated to a more differentiated state (to use biological terminology). A little reflection indicates that there are two main aspects to epistemology, which we may briefly characterize as "psychological" and "physical." The psychological side of epistemology is no doubt the older one: How does the human mind or consciousness create a picture of the outside world and how is this picture related to the structure and activity of the mind? In our inquiry, however, we are not concerned with this form of epistemology. The second aspect, which we have just called physical epistemology, made its appearance, historically speaking, only after the concept of general, empirically verifiable natural laws conceived as abstract relationships had been sufficiently established. The question is then: How far can one generalize from known, observable regularities; how much universality can one ascribe to the laws of nature and to the phenomena which they imply? One may consider David Hume as perhaps the most important early thinker on physical epistemology. His conclusions are very clear and definite: Logical and probabilistic *induction* is the method of generalization, and induction by its very nature is only an estimate and can never acquire the mathematical rigor of a deductive scheme.

Throughout history, some of the most distinguished scientists have brushed aside epistemological qualms; they were what professional philosophers choose to call "naïve realists." They claimed that the external world can be described exhaustively in terms of definite sets of numbers (or functions); these numbers constitute reality and there is little else to be said by way of philosophical interpretation. In the course of the development of classical physics this simplified view has been eminently useful in keeping scientists away from many philosophical subtleties which were unnecessary at that stage. Even so, it appeared that implicit, unwarranted assumptions arising out of traditional ways of thought tended to slip into scientific description without our realizing it. The positivistic school of scientific philosophy which flourished in the late nineteenth and early twentieth centuries concentrated on ferreting out these implicit assumptions and did so with remarkable success. Much of modern theoretical physics and in particular the theory of relativity stands as a monument to the tremendous results achieved.

History, however, often moves in devious ways. One would think that Humean empirical criticism in its interaction with the naïve realists would have kept the philosophers of science busy for a long stretch. But nothing so simple occurred. The main emphasis of natural philosophy in the eighteenth and nineteenth centuries was on the rigid validity of a precise determinism of the Newtonian style. This clearly leads to the conception of a purely mechanistic, clockwork-type universe (usually connected with the name of Laplace). But the impact of the extreme rationalism of the early eighteenth century upon its contemporary society had been excessive, and there arose a certain reaction. One of its chief representatives in the realm of abstract thought was Kant.

He starts out by positing dogmatically that rigid Newtonian causality must reign throughout the physical world. He then declares that the idea of such a clockwork universe is incompatible with his moral sensibilities. He tries to resolve the conflict by effecting what may well be called a forced marriage between physical and psychological epistemology. He claims that the external world, being meaningless without an observing subject, is filtered through the mind of the subject, and in this filtering process the contradictions can be made to disappear (the details to be left to students of Kant's philosophy) .

The reader of these pages may by now be quite exasperated with this digression into pure philosophy. Its purpose is, however, a very precise one. Kant's philosophy has had a powerful influence, and, in central Europe especially, it has stayed alive well into our times. This fact has had repercussions at the time of the greatest advances in atomic physics. The development of quantum mechanics differed from that of other physical theories in that there was no pre-existing conceptual scheme which could later be formulated in mathematical terms. Instead, the situation was somewhat the reverse; the original discoveries were largely mathematical, and a suitable scheme of interpretation had thereupon to be formed. It was exactly at this point that the founders of quantum theory made use of the Kantian philosophy, which happened to be conveniently at hand and widely known. Unfortunately, these efforts at hybridizing atomic physics and Kantian philosophy have to our knowledge never been critically revised. Thus if we read in a text on the interpretation of quantum theory that the physical interaction between a measuring device and a measured object corresponds to the relationship between the observing subject and the observed object we are not dealing with any straightforward consequence of the formal theory; what we are seeing is in fact a version of Kantian philosophy. There is nothing in the nature of the observations or the structure of the theory that would compel us to think along these particular lines; their significance derives essentially from historical circumstances.

We do not doubt that in some remote future when we know a great deal about the dynamics of the brain, the psychological and the physical aspects of epistemology can be brought together again, but this is not at all the situation with which we are now confronted. At the present stage of development, an epistemology pertaining to the more physical aspects of science must be based on the methodology of *physical* science, and the mainstay of this methodology is *inductive inference*. We may if we wish distinguish two types of inductive inference: that which is universal and terminal, leading to the recognition of natural law (e.g., the laws of quantum mechanics), and that which is special and contingent, leading to probabilistic estimates of microscopic structure if certain measurements of macrovariables are given. It is with the latter type of problem that we are more especially concerned.

Lest the reader be led to believe, however, that we are again introducing a subjectivistic element, although perhaps not Kantian, let us remark that we in no way claim that one can speak of macrovariables only when they have been measured by a specific observer. The macrovariables ought to be considered in the tradition of classical physics in terms of naïve realism, that is, as constituting in an objective sense the elements of the external world. What is in question here is the relationship of the microstates to the macrovariables. The mathematical details of this problem can only be treated by means of the methods of statistical mechanics (see for instance Elsasser, 1962a).

2 · 9

The author has found as a result of many years of experience that one cannot develop a satisfactory scheme of theoretical biology without passing first through certain of these critical problems of epistemology. This does not of course mean that the biologist in his daily work ought to concern himself with philosophy; far from it. Philosophy here resembles the compass which tells us where West is if this is the direction in which we can get out of the woods. Provided we have other means to ascertain that we are moving in a straight line, not in circles, we do not have to look constantly at the compass.

The epistemological difficulties which arise in biological theory stem directly from the fact that the precise microscopic state of a macroscopic system such as an organism can only be known *inferentially*. This is implied in the basic consequence of quantum theory first recognized by Bohr: that the precise determination of a microstate by multiple observations introduces disturbances which would totally disrupt the system at hand. Hence for most purposes we have to abstain from such thoroughgoing observations. If we do so we must admit to a large degree of indeterminacy in the description of the microscopic structure of a system that has a certain size and complexity. If one uses this indeterminacy to appeal to philosophical subjectivism (as is done by surreptitiously introducing elements of Kant's philosophy into science in the manner criticized in Section 2.8) then the road to a rational theoretical biology is barred. It is therefore imperative that one try to consider indeterminacy in the conditions of material bodies as an objective state of affairs. This can be done by starting from the macrovariables which we may assume objectively given, and using only inductive inferences. The argument involved here is one of method, and hence the acceptable criterion is, plainly, success. In a successful theory *indeterminacy must be given an objective meaning in terms of inductive inferences.*

The inductive process is not used indiscriminately in our context but proceeds in two steps. There is first the inductive generalization of those experiences that are condensed into the laws of quantum mechanics, which we assume valid whether the object is living or not. This is a postulate in the nature of a working hypothesis. It would have to come under scrutiny only if there should appear distinct evidence to the effect that it is false. Now the laws of quantum mechanics provide in general only necessary conditions for the phenomena and not sufficient ones, that is, they do not uniquely determine the happenings on the microscopic level. Hence there remains a large field for inductive inference, and it is with this type of inference that we are concerned. The primary data here consist of a set of macrovariables combined into a given system event. The inferences are indeterminate for several reasons. In the first place, there is the purely probabilistic assignment of microstates corresponding to the fact that an immense number of them is available. Secondly there is the intrinsic ambiguity of all inductive inference, there being no universal rule as to a "best" way of using this tool. Thirdly there is the vagueness springing from the fact that the transition from the macroscopic to the microscopic variables is a gradual one and no sharp boundary between the two exists.

To say that a system *is* in a given microscopic state

and that we just happen not to know what this state is, represents an operationally meaningless proposition. It would be equivalent to the following assumed statement applying to atomic theory: In a hydrogen atom the electron *is* at any specific moment in a specific spatial position relative to the nucleus, but not having measured it we cannot tell where it is. In both instances one has overlooked the fact that before the measurement(s) the object was representative of a certain class or classes; but the classes representative of the conditions before and after the measurement are quite different from each other. To appreciate this one should keep in mind that science deals with propositions about classes and not with individuals outside of their being representatives of classes. We claim, furthermore, that the statistical indeterminacy of quantum mechanics and the indeterminacy of the inductive inferences discussed here are closely related and as a rule cannot even be separated from each other. They can be separated clearly only in the limiting case where a system has first been prepared to be represented by a well-defined single wave function.

Those acquainted with quantum theory will realize that a wave function (more precisely its square) does not represent the probability that an object, for instance an electron, is somewhere in space. Instead, a wave function is always a functional relationship between *two* variables, one of them having a definite value (the eigenvalue) and the other corresponding to a probability distribution. In the language of probability theory, a wave function defines a *conditional* probability. Effectively all epistemological difficulties result from overlooking this fact. We require as a rule a specific experimental setup to bring a system into a condition where it is represented by a single wave function or a very narrow bundle of them (for instance in an atomic beam experiment). In the absence of such a specialized arrangement which experimentally isolates a single wave function, *both* variables are statistically indeterminate and must as a rule remain so in highly complex systems as long as one refrains from wholly destructive measuring operations. Under these circumstances one is almost automatically led to a description in terms of the models of statistical mechanics, that is, of ensembles, in which only the macrovariables have determinate values.

2·10

The reader will now undoubtedly ask how the preceding semi-philosophical arguments can be related to the widely accepted interpretation of biology in purely mechanistic "molecular" terms, often referred to as "reductionism" (the reduction of biological phenomena to physics and chemistry). We intend to show that the nature of this relationship can be clarified to a rather high degree; we shall attack this task in two steps.

In the first place it seems very clear, it is almost a platitude in fact, that Nature is a far better engineer than any human being. Thus we can quite safely expect that any repetitive process in the organism will be found to be mechanized or automated to an extreme degree. Such automatization characterizes as a general rule the dynamics of what we have previously called the homogeneous components of the organism, primarily the organic macromolecules which constitute the main subject matter of what is called molecular biology. The processes undergone by these molecules commonly take place according to rules of straightforward causality, based on definite chemical relationships. To adduce just one example: the denaturation of protein molecules is often a reversible process; re-naturation, that is, the coiling up of the proteins into extremely complicated but perfectly well-defined three-dimensional patterns, occurs under certain thermal and electrochemical conditions; these precise conformations turn out to be necessary for many enzymatic actions of proteins. However, it would be effectively impossible in practice to predict these determinate processes from such knowledge of macromolecular structure as we have at our disposal. Similar processes of restitution can occur in other protein substances, for instance collagen. It is clear that a great variety of chemically determinate processes are extremely widespread in the dynamics of the homogeneous components of the organism, that is, in macromolecular chemical kinetics. Furthermore, there is no reason at all to think that more than a small fraction of the mechanisms of this kind is already known to us; the future undoubtedly holds numerous surprises; molecular biologists will hardly run out of material for the study of the intriguing, causally determinate mechanisms whereby the living organism contrives to use its homogeneous components for the performance of repetitive operations.

The question we need to answer is whether the activities of the organism can for all practical purposes be subsumed under the causal functioning of its homogeneous components. An engineer who is an expert in the operation of assembly lines and who is studying an industrialized society is inclined to lay great stress on the variety and ubiquity of assembly lines; he might well be inclined to underestimate the role of the other functions in the economic system which he studies. Perhaps, on looking at the organism primarily in terms of the obvious fundamental significance of the molecular dynamics of its homogeneous components, one may be inclined to fall prey to a similar distortion of view.

2 · 11

We now come to a second critical point. We have spoken before of the indeterminacy in the microstates of a system which is reasonably large (on the atomic-molecular scale) and complex. At first sight we are confronted here with a seeming contradiction. On the one hand there is, we claim, this microscopic indeterminacy, on the other we also see precise, causally determinate processes occurring among the homogeneous components, and these processes are to all appearances highly reproducible. How can this contradiction be understood?

Starting from the concept of microscopic indeterminacy, it is important to keep in mind one aspect of it. One might ask whether there is any specific scale along which indeterminacy increases more and more. Of course there is no assurance that any scale exists, and we do not think that one can in fact find a precise one. But one might suppose that in a rough approximation a scale is furnished by geometrical dimension: the smaller the objects at hand the less determinate the way in which they can be related to the macrovariables. But even a mild familiarity with the facts of atomic and molecular physics will show that this is not so. Experience shows that the only possible basis for a scale of this kind is not geometrical dimensions but energy. The smaller the energy, the more it is to be expected that statistical elements will enter into the determination of the microscopic state relative to the macrovariables.

To illustrate this, consider the average energy *per*

atom in a complex system such as organic tissue. It is of course well known that by far the largest energies occur in the chemical bonds of saturated molecules. As a result, these molecules and the geometrical conformations associated with their bonds are extremely stable. This stability is precisely what we described before as the main feature of the homogeneous components of organisms. Take for instance a simple organic molecule such as some sugar molecule or one of its derivatives. We may be able to establish fairly readily (for instance by optical means) that a certain number of such molecules are contained in a given volume. But it would be infinitely more difficult to determine the precise location or orientation of these molecules on a sufficiently refined microscopic scale. The latter task would involve following their diffusive motions and would lead us immediately into a realm of small energies, often hundreds of times smaller than the binding energies of stable molecules.

It is within the domain of these *small* energies that we have to look for the immense variability of admissible microstates. There are a number of forms of molecular interactions in which these small energies appear: First of all the energy of thermal agitation which gives rise to diffusion processes. These are invariably complicated in biological material because cells contain both aqueous and lipid components. On a level slightly above the thermal one there are the energies of surface attraction (van der Waals forces) between molecules which give rise to associations, to adsorption at membranes, and so on. There are the energies of electrostatic polarization of ions at some distance from each other. The known, exceptionally high mobility of free protons may well have a significance for biochemical kinetics which has not yet been fully explored (see also Elsasser, 1962b). In this connection one cannot fail to mention a configurational change which is so common in organic tissue, that is, the resonant interchange of single and double bonds that constantly takes place in the innumerable organic molecules which have conjugated bonds. This process is very rapid and requires no external energy transfer for an isolated molecule, but it might require minute energies if different parts of the molecule are subject to varying external forces. The number of conjugated bonds in the constituent molecules of organic tissue is so large that an elementary calculation shows the number of possible bond configurations in even a fractional volume of a living cell to be immense in our precise sense of the word.

Moreover, when we speak of chemical changes we should remember that the enzymatically induced reactions in living tissue do not as a general rule involve an irreversible dissipation of large amounts of energy. The reactions are coupled and balanced in such a way that the *net* dissipation of energy is small: one reaction partner may lose a large amount of energy while the other partner gains nearly as much, so that only the small difference is dissipated in heat.

Hence there exists in living tissue an immense number of configurational arrangements which differ from each other by only small energies, these energy differences being as a rule either of thermal order or else of a magnitude a few times thermal energy. From our viewpoint, this immense reservoir of microstates has a double meaning. When looked at under the aspect of interpretation (or epistemology) it indicates the presence of an immense microscopic indeterminacy which can only be treated statistically within the context of inductive inferences. On the other hand, this variability coexists with the stability of the saturated molecules, including of course the macromolecules, which constitute what we have called the homogeneous components. Their lifetime in the absence of enzymatically mediated reactions would be almost unlimited on the scale of cellular processes.

Our problem here is not that of the mere distinction between these two types of energy levels, since the relevant facts have been overwhelmingly established by observation. The essential problem concerns the degree of *coupling* between them. This brings us to the second interpretation of the immense number of the microstates and the ever-present transitions between them in living tissue. (These transitions would almost disappear, of course, if the material were frozen and metabolism stopped.) The coupling of these small-energy transitions into major energy exchanges or chemical rearrangements among otherwise stable molecules is what in common engineering parlance is called *noise*. (It is true that noise will here not have the exact meaning that it usually does for the engineer or physicist, who is wont to think implicitly in terms of homogeneous systems and their representation by homogeneous classes. In these, all statistical averages and with them all statistical distribution functions without exception have a well-defined mathematical meaning. This is not the case in a universe of finite, radically inhomogeneous classes, where many such averages which involve microscopic quantities cannot be properly defined. Fortunately, for the purpose of the present argument it is possible to disregard the distinction between homogeneous and inhomogeneous classes and to deal with the problem simply as the effect of noise upon the chemical transformations of the homogeneous components.)

2·12

If one looks at these chemical transformations from the viewpoint of a purely mechanistic interpretation of the processes of molecular biology, one must assume that the feedback-stabilized transformations (including especially replications) of the macromolecules are very carefully uncoupled from the noise level. It appears entirely legitimate to compare the situation to that prevailing in an electronic computer, where there are two distinct dynamical levels: that of the signals (information) and that of noise. The designer of computers aims at minimizing the influence of noise, since noise is a statistical phenomenon and the effect of it upon the information is invariably deleterious; it always diminishes the amount of information available (Shannon's generalization of the second law to information theory). We shall not stop to justify the application of information-theoretical concepts to the transformations, especially replication of organic macromolecules. This application seems legitimate within reason and is no doubt well enough known in its general terms to the reader, as it is discussed in a qualitative fashion at many places in the literature. The requirements for decoupling deleterious noise from the regular processes of macromolecular reproduction are extremely stringent. Thus in a recent review on the self-replication mechanism of DNA in *E. coli*, Pollard (1965) states that an "error rate" of the general order of 10^{-8} is required to ensure sufficiently precise replication in the long run. Even for a carefully designed electronic computer with solid-state components an overall error rate of one part in a hundred million is respectably small, to say the least. Pollard's figure is by no means exceptional; it must rather be considered typical (to within one or two powers of ten) of the error rates at which students of this problem have repeatedly arrived. Results of this type suggest that the organism must go to extreme pains in shielding or buffering the information contained in the macromolecules from chemical noise. Evidence for the existence of suitable buffering devices has so far not been discovered. Commoner (1964 a and b) has developed in some detail a model of the chemical feedback cycles involved in the replication of DNA, and this model shows the replication process, by way of the enzymes required, to be tied into the pool of amino acids, whose concentrations appear as parameters of the problem. Under these conditions error rates of the order mentioned must indeed appear exceedingly low.

It is clear, on the other hand, that there should be a mechanistic aspect to the problem of reducing noise interference in macromolecular transformations. On general grounds one may expect a mechanism to exist whenever a *repetitive* process in the organism is to be performed. In connection with the transmission of a genetic code it is most appropriate to think of the pertinent mechanisms under the form of error-correcting devices. Such devices have been studied by computer theorists with very interesting results. In this connection there is universal agreement about one basic fact: the only way the deterioration of information by noise can be prevented, or at least reduced, is by means of redundancy, that is, the presence of the same information several times over. An automaton, on comparing several versions of an information sequence with each other, can correct those occasional ones which differ from all the others. On this basis von Neumann (1956) designed a theoretical system of error-correcting automata using a method of "multiplexing" components. He was able to show that in this manner the total average error of the automaton as a whole can in principle be made as low as one wishes, much lower than the average error committed by any one component of the machine. Von Neumann found, however, that the degree of redundancy or multiplicity needed to achieve a really low error rate is exceedingly large, and so the size of the mechanism required for low error rates is likely to be prohibitive. The problem was taken up again more recently by Winograd and Cowan (1963), who showed that von Neumann's automaton can be much improved upon. A systematic application of the results of information theory proves that one can design automata in which the information is more widely distributed, in such a way as to make the effect of noise upon some part of the information less deleterious, with a corresponding very large saving in the number of components required. Still, it seems certain that for the repeated and reasonably error-free processing of a body of information of some size quite large and complex automata are required.

The value of the preceding, seemingly somewhat remote arguments lies in the fact that to the approximation in which the living cell functions mechanistically it is, by all the evidence available, an information-processing device. Chemical knowledge, intricate as it is, does not seem enough; general models of information transfer and its error rates, as they have been considered by information theorists such as the authors quoted, are essential. Unfortunately, we find the latter kind of analysis still in a very early stage of development so far as its applications are concerned. In particular, its application to the chemical dynamics of the cell appears quite some distance in the future. It is not too much to think, however, that the basic question, the problem of the coupling of the information contained in the macromolecules to noise, might eventually be capable of an operational decision. Criteria can no doubt be established for the minimum coupling that can be tolerated if the two separate worlds so characteristic of mechanistic biology, that of chemically coded information and that of chemical noise, are to exist next to each other without degradation of the information content of the cell over the time required for untold cell divisions.

We must guard here against interpreting the meaning of an operational decision in too limited a way. Biology is the domain of the utterly complex, and hence we can not expect that a decision would be so clear-cut as to be in terms of one simple experiment, a procedure of a kind that is so often sufficient to resolve controversies of physics or chemistry. A variety of more or less complicated experiments may be required, interlaced by theoretical reasoning. Still, one must certainly be quite wary of too early conclusions. Limited experimental results that show certain molecular transformations less reliable than anticipated will of course prove nothing so long as the total mechanism is not adequately understood. The general view to which we adhere in this book does not carry in it any means of short-circuiting a thorough analysis along purely mechanistic lines.

2 · 13

It will also appear from the preceding that we have to distinguish clearly between two aspects in the application of the information concept to biology. There is extensive storage of information in the germ cell, in fact in any cell, with DNA as the carrier of the long-term purely static storage. If this storage did not exist biology would be hopelessly dualistic. We would be forced to the primitive animistic assumption that there is some sort of agency acting in the germ cell which spurs the organization of its material during the developmental process.

On the other hand, there is the problem as to what happens to the information while it is being processed, that is, utilized in transformations which create intermediate or terminal structures quite different from the structures in which information had been stored to begin with. *Information is most vulnerable and most susceptible to modification while it is being processed*, not when it is in storage. This statement, familiar to any designer of computers, is quite general and is not critically dependent on the nature of the mechanisms or processes involved in the manipulation of information. Nor does it seem to depend on a rigorous definition of biological information at this stage of the inquiry. However, one has every reason to presume that a more clear-cut definition will emerge as the understanding of biochemical kinetics proceeds. One must avoid a purely static interpretation of information in the biological context: the stored information corresponds to the initial conditions of a dynamical system, and with respect to this dynamics the initial conditions are only one element. By far the most difficult problem here is the analysis of the detailed dynamics of the transformations themselves. To assume that everything that happens is uniquely determined by the initial conditions is of course to pre-empt the whole issue in favor of a purely mechanistic interpretation. Even in basic problems of physics, infinitely less complicated than any problem of biology, this is an overly simplistic approach. Recently, the distinguished physicist L. Brillouin (1964) has devoted a book to this very problem as it appears within the confines of physics proper. Even in the realm of purely "classical" physics, the relationship of the state of a system to its initial con-

· 101 ·

ditions is often far more tenuous than our deep-rooted tradition of a purely deterministic view of the physical world would lead one to believe. After the treatment given it by Brillouin, that old stand-by of deterministic epistemology, the "Laplacian spirit," which can measure everything with any desired accuracy and then make corresponding predictions, seems rather badly battered even in its home area, that of purely classical physics.

CHAPTER 3 · THE MEANING
OF LOGICAL COMPLEXITY

3·1

We have seen that one of the most characteristic features of organisms, perhaps their most outstanding one, is their utter complexity in structure as well as in function. The existence of this complexity suggests a line of thought to which biologists in the past have not always given suitable emphasis. True, the concept involved is often implicitly indicated, but rarely do we find it explicitly and precisely exhibited with all its consequences. It is the idea that, most likely, a basic aspect of biological relationships is *intrinsic and irreducible logical complexity*. By this we mean that due to the absence of pervasive rigid categories (binary answers to questions, see Chapter 1) it may not be possible to resolve complicated relationships of order into a set of comparatively simple ones each of which can be separately studied, after which they can be composed so as to account successfully for the behavior of the system as a whole. (Note that we speak here of rather general logical relationships, not just of a part-whole relation as in feedback cycles, which can be quite simply analyzed in mechanistic terms.) The famous Cartesian method, which enjoins us to break a complicated problem down into simple component problems and to study these one by one, constitutes a piece of advice that tells us how to go about scientific inquiries and as such must of course forever go unchallenged, but it is not a prescription on Nature. Now we are not thinking here of a rather superficial use, or misuse, of a notion such as causality, as when somebody tells us that some process occurs in the organism "because" certain chemical reaction partners are present and next tells us that the process occurs also "because" evolution has provided a mechanism for it. This would be no more than careless and uncritical application of everyday language. More is involved.

There are clearly innumerable processes in the organism which can be understood in terms of mechanistic models. But can these models be made exhaustive? Can the conditions be made both necessary and sufficient? Consider a simple example from physical science. A chemical reaction may be well known, its mechanism may be thoroughly studied and considered as understood. But one day somebody finds that the reaction does require a catalyst which in all past experiments has been present in minute amounts without the knowledge of the experimenters. Here we have a presumptive and approximate understanding of a natural process which turns out later to be incomplete.

The problem which concerns us in this book is how the assumed autonomous aspects of the behavior of organisms may be related to the mechanistic ones. We may find the situation to be so complex that we would need many samples to elucidate it in detail, and we may then find that we run out of members of the class considered before a question regarding some regularities of their mutual relationship has been decided. This argument illustrates (perhaps better, it defines) the nature of irreducible logical complexity. The case of a single such question is of course too simple; we must rather think of sets of such questions when we deal with the intricate regularities of biology. It appears that intrinsic logical complexity becomes scientifically significant as a property of finite, inhomogeneous classes. Traditional biological generalizations are frequently far from this view. Thus mechanistic biological philosophy tries to reduce the complex behavior of the organism to the much simpler laws of physics; vitalism on the other hand tries to explain organisms in terms of the quasi-physical concept of a superadded vital force.

3 · 2

It stands to reason that the organism is in the first approximation, and foremost, a rather complex system of physico-chemical machinery. To consider the organism apart from its mechanistic components and functions is patently absurd. This is such a fundamental fact that one must be quite sure not to mistake it for an implicit guarantee that mechanistic biology will be successful by itself. However, since our concern is here with the non-mechanistic aspects of biology, we feel compelled to dwell on this fact with some force: *A concept of life outside or apart from a specific set of physico-chemical mechanisms is completely meaningless*; life can be described satisfactorily only if one starts with an analysis of the physico-chemical mechanisms of which every living being is composed. Our contention is that the understanding of the mechanistic processes is a prerequisite for a broader analysis of the functioning of the organism that arises, not through the operation of some separate agency but as a result of the radical inhomogeneity of the microscopic state of the system combined with its intrinsic indeterminacy.

A pervasive asymmetry is thus seen to be characteristic of the relationship of mechanistic to autonomous components in the organism's dynamics. This asymmetry corresponds precisely to that prevailing between the macrovariables and the immense reservoir of microstates. Very often the macrovariables can be considered by themselves, and, according to the laws of classical physics and chemistry, their mutual relationships can be analyzed in determinate form for some finite length of time (until, that is, the coupling into the inhomogeneous microstates begins to make precise analysis and corresponding prediction impossible). The fact that the relationship of the mechanistic to the autonomous process components is dependent upon, and therefore largely patterned after, the physical relationship of macrovariables and microstates has been the origin of many of the difficulties and misconceptions which have arisen in biological theorizing. The tendency of so many investigators who are concerned with specific macroscopic mechanisms to make short shrift of any organismic concepts, and to generalize mechanistic views too readily beyond their original limits, can no doubt be traced to this source.

Now from the preceding arguments we can draw a conclusion of great importance. If the autonomous components of organismic behavior cannot exist by themselves but can act only by way of the coupling of the radically inhomogeneous but at the same time indeterminate microstructure into the macrovariables, then one may also expect that *there exist no abstract and general principles* which could be applied to the autonomy of organisms, considered as a phenomenon of its own. In other words, there should be no general laws of "pure" biology; whatever laws there are can be formulated only in relation to specific physico-chemical mechanisms which are realized in more or less extensive classes of organisms. We need hardly say that this is an explicit application of the idea of intrinsic logical complexity outlined above. A perusal of much of the material of observational biology shows our presumption— the non-existence of "general" biological laws which would be dissociated from specific mechanisms—to be indeed fulfilled; we shall revert to this proposition later on and give examples for it.

Since the autonomy of the modes of behavior is therefore always relative, and incomprehensible apart from the mechanisms into which the indeterminate, radically inhomogeneous substratum is coupled, we should properly always speak of *semi*-autonomy. If on occasion we speak just of autonomy, the reader will understand that this is no more than a convenient abbreviation of speech.

3 · 3

We note that in dealing with semi-autonomy of the kind described we are faced with a certain degree of conceptual novelty in the following sense: In the history of physical science at least, efforts at theory construction have almost invariably tended to take one of two alternative courses. Either the fundamental laws were assumed as given and novel types of precise deductions from them were sought, as in the case of the kinetic theory of matter, where atoms or molecules were assumed to obey mechanical laws of motion, and new and on the surface quite distinct properties, in this case the laws of heat and thermodynamics, were derived from them. This same scheme applies to all of classical physiology, where time and again investigators have succeeded in interpreting aspects of the behavior of organisms by the application of well-established principles of physics and chemistry.

The second case which has repeatedly occurred in the history of physical science is that certain laws of physics that were meant to apply to a limited domain had, outside this domain, to be modified, both mathematically and conceptually, to obtain a novel theory. This is clearly so with quantum physics, where Newtonian mechanics remains valid for macroscopic phenomena, but as we descend into the microscopic domain, the realm of atoms and molecules, these classical concepts fail and a new theory, quantitatively different from the old one, takes over.

The time-honored dualism of mechanistic and vitalistic concepts in biology expresses the notion that the observed biological regularities are either logico-mathematically derivable from the laws of atomic and molecular physics or else require specific modification of these laws. Our present theory does not agree with either of these ideas. We base ourselves upon the vast extent of inhomogeneity combined with statistical indeterminacy of microstates and the attendant lack of predictability, and we assume that this indeterminacy is an essential precondition of the partially autonomous behavior of organisms. (The other condition, as we hardly need to repeat, is the validity of the principle of finite classes.) A theory of this type which is based on inadequate determinacy within the existing theory, rather than on any modification of it as proposed by the vitalists, is here designated as *organismic*. This term has in the past primarily been used by biologists who approached the problem from an essentially global, observational point of view; hence we should consider first of all certain aspects of our abstract scheme that are more clearly than others related to an empirically oriented view.

3·4

When the observing biologist speaks of organismic properties he invariably has in mind what he calls phenomena of "integration" or of "integrative" behavior. He tells us that although he is not prepared to admit any modifications of the basic laws of molecular physics and chemistry, he finds in organisms a type of behavior which, without violating these laws, appears to give to the organism an aspect of "wholeness" whose origin in physics he has every right to consider as being rather obscure. Some of the observed behavior is no doubt due to stabilization by feedback arrangements, chemical or otherwise. But we agree here with those biologists who claim that not all of the stability and regularity of organisms can be so explained.

We are now prepared to formulate a basically different approach to the problem of "biological integration." We propose that what appears as such integration (and therefore is so often attributed to some "vital forces") *can be wholly expressed in terms of the relationship of the individual to the class.*

We shall try to explain what is meant by this after some preliminaries. First, we remember that each system event is equivalent to an immensely rare occurrence among an immense number of possible ones. Immensely rare events in a radically inhomogeneous substratum are those which we expect to have minimal predictability. If we start from the macrovariables of a given system event, our predictions become the more uncertain and diffuse the further we want to extrapolate into the future. But what we actually find in organisms is a definite sequence of patterns, be it stability of an individual organism, developmental stages, or the like. (Let us recall here that we previously agreed to take as the members of our classes the system events, that is, organisms at given instants of time. This purely formal device permits us to think of a single organism considered over a lengthy period of time as a sequence of system events; from this viewpoint the organism in space-time appears itself as a class. Often of course we do not want to deal with just one organism but will include as members of the class system events that pertain to numerous individuals of, say, the same species.)

A mechanistic biology makes operational sense only if

it can tell us that any system event can be adequately predicted from preceding system events by application of the laws of physics. What we find in nature is the extraordinary stability of classes; we see these classes maintain their characteristics in great detail over untold generations. In figurative language we can express this by saying that out of an immense number of possible processes leading from one system event to subsequent ones, the organism "selects" those processes that ensure the stability of the class. "Selection" is of course purely a convenience of speech; it does not here presuppose a selecting agency but only expresses in alternate language the stability of classes to that degree in which it is an autonomous phenomenon: out of an immense number of possible transformations from one system event to a later one only an immensely small fraction is actually realized, and these represent the stable properties of the class. The fact that we are thus always dealing with immensely rare events precludes our being able to derive the corresponding prediction wholly from physical laws; it precludes also that we could ever arrive at a contradiction with these laws.

Again, it is no accident that so many distinguished observing biologists have proposed a failure of the second law of thermodynamics in the organism. This is exactly what the matter looks like at the surface; it is the simplest way of interpreting the phenomenon of biological integration, provided one does not wish to modify the basic laws of motion, those of (quantum) mechanics. From the statistical viewpoint the second law expresses a very general tendency of any system of sufficient complexity to change in the direction of increased disorder, and the abrogation of this law would in fact be equivalent to postulating implicitly some sort of ordering principle. But in our theory such a scheme would have no operational meaning, since such deviations from the second law could not be verified: The "selection" of certain immensely rare processes which ensure the stability of classes is withdrawn from direct observation.

3 · 5

The autonomy, or semi-autonomy, of the classes of biology in the sense just explained might at first sight appear a somewhat strange notion. It carries with it, of course, the explicit denial of "forces," "fields," or other principles of extensionality going in any way beyond those implied in a conventional physical analysis, that is, the denial of any quasi-physical, superadded agencies suitable for generating and maintaining the relative similarity of system events that pertain to the same class but are separated in space or time. Of course, this organismic autonomy is always only partial, because each organism has first of all its mechanistic aspects in respect to which it functions according to well-established physical laws, and some of these mechanisms subserve stability.

In developing this concept of the semi-autonomy of biological classes we have modeled our ideas upon the autonomy of the classes of atomic physics. The physicist has every confidence in his belief that two hydrogen atoms, say, separated in space and in time, are exactly alike to the point of being completely indistinguishable and interchangeable. This class concept cannot be derived from the principles of extensionality; there are no forces or other physical interactions among atoms of the same class that would modify them, so that they are found identical to each other; their identity is a primary fact of nature. In fact, if one tries to analyze the mutual independence of the postulates which are required to establish the laws of atomic physics, *the logically primitive character of the class concept* soon becomes apparent.

The idea of the semi-autonomy of biological classes is thus far based on analogy to atomic physics. An analogy of this kind can and must be pushed much further. To appreciate this, we shall first compare the quantum-mechanical model of an atom, say the hydrogen atom, with a model based on classical, Newtonian physics as it was earlier developed by Rutherford. In that scheme the electron was assumed to circulate about the proton in the manner of a planet circulating about the sun. While such a model accounts for many properties of atoms in a semi-quantitative way, it has one radical defect. The electron, having a charge, must radiate in a curved orbit, and hence it loses energy continuously. It therefore spirals gradually inward and ends up by falling into the nucleus. Within the framework of classical physics no remedy for this inadequacy of the model has ever been found. In other words, models of classical physics can never account for the *stability* of atoms (or molecules). In quantum theory on the other hand we have sharply defined levels that are stable for limited times and a ground state which is stable indefinitely. This is made possible by the novel characteristics of the electron which let it partake of the properties of a corpuscle and at the same time of those of a wave, the duality expressed mathematically in the Heisenberg uncertainty relations. As is well known, these relations imply that we cannot have as exhaustive a knowledge of the motion of the electron as we would have in a classical model. Niels Bohr, in his efforts at a concrete physical and conceptual interpretation of quantum theory, has never ceased to emphasize that it is this *restriction of knowledge*, that is, of definiteness within a scheme of extensionality, which makes the stability of atoms and of molecules meaningful within the new theory. We are not, then, given an "explanation" of the stability in terms of some appropriate mechanical contrivance; instead, this stability is part of the autonomy of atomic systems, this autonomy being understood as relative to classical, Newtonian physics.

What Bohr's ideas indicate in a broader context is that if we find properties of natural objects which cannot be subsumed under a mechanistic scheme and which therefore make the behavior of these objects appear relatively autonomous, then *we should in the first place look for fundamental restrictions on the possible knowledge of the objects*; these restrictions are then correlative to the autonomy encountered in the objects. Hence as soon as one admits that organisms have autonomous aspects, this approach leads one to look for intrinsic restrictions on the possible knowledge of the detailed structure and dynamics of organisms. The autonomy of organisms will then be correlative to the intrinsic restriction of knowledge rather than being dependent on any modification of the laws of physics that would be expressed by some organizing, vital principle.

Now we have found above that there exist indeed severe and inescapable restrictions on knowledge in the study of organisms. We recognized that a system as complex as an organism cannot be represented by a single wave function of quantum theory, as can the ground state of an atom, say. Instead, we are forced to use methods of statistical mechanics in such a way that only the macrovariables have specified values. This representation involves immense numbers of microstates among which we cannot discriminate on the basis of the given macrovariables; the description is only in terms of inductive probabilities with respect to an immense bundle of microstates that cannot be ascertained individually. The limitation of knowledge which concerns us here, and which we assume to be correlative with the semi-autonomy of biological classes, is therefore the uncertainty of microscopic detail of the type dealt with by statistical mechanics.

We remark finally that ever since the notion of complementarity was introduced into physics some forty years ago, the mere term has on many occasions been used uncritically in attempts to rejuvenate past dualisms which are often much better left to the silence of ancient tomes resting on library shelves. Our present generalization of the complementarity concept to biology is highly specific, being closely analogous to the mode of thought of atomic physics. Now while the relationship of limitation of knowledge to autonomy constitutes the core of any concept of the "complementarity" type, it is *only* in quantum mechanics that this limitation is built directly into the universal laws of motion and interaction. On a higher level, in biology, we could also speak of "complementarity," but the term must then be interpreted in a different sense, relating to statistical mechanics, as just described. We think it better to restrict the term complementarity to quantum mechanics proper, and in the case underlying biological autonomy to speak of *organismic relationships.*

3 · 6

The scheme of abstract thought which we have sketched in the foregoing might be characterized alternatively by saying that it involves an *intuitional paradox,* or perhaps paradoxes. In coining this term we certainly do not imply an internal logical contradiction or inconsistency; such would be intolerable in any theory whatever. What we have in mind is a clash of scientific ideas with what may be considered in a given situation as reasonable, obvious, representing common sense, and so on. These latter notions are invariably the expression of long-ingrained, thoroughly established modes of thought; in other words they represent, to a very large extent, habit. Again, this does not mean that such ideas can be completely subsumed under habit or training. Since the earlier forms of science attach themselves quite closely to direct macroscopic observations of our environment they also may be closely related (at least in part) to genetically determined modes of reaction of our central nervous system.

The history of physics offers numerous examples for the appearance of intuitional paradoxes. It may be advantageous to look at these next in a historical context rather than to dwell on purely abstract relationships. Galileo emancipated physics by showing that the traditional concept of a state of absolute rest needed to be abandoned and that, instead, all coordinate systems that are in uniform motion relative to each other (inertial systems) are physically equivalent or, as we would say in present-day language, operationally indistinguishable. Here, for the first time, appears the basic notion that abstract scientific models are to be defined in such a way that their content appears as a consequence of mutual relationships of their constituents in place of their being related to some Absolute. The idea implicit here, that the elements of an abstract structure are to be defined by their mutual relationships within the structure and not by reference to some external entities, has formed the basis of the method of scientific theory ever since.

Galileo's ideas must certainly have appeared to his contemporaries as very close to what we have termed above an intuitional paradox. But even before Galileo, students of the natural sciences were faced with the difficulty of reconciling with their intuitive understanding the fact that since the earth is round the antipodes appear to themselves as walking upright, and they do not fall off the earth into the void. We are told that some less imaginative naturalists objected to this idea occasionally even as late as the early eighteenth century.

It was upon the acceptance of these two early samples of intuitional paradoxes that Newton's synthesis expressed in his laws of mechanics and gravitation was based. With this, the chasm was crossed, and we find a very long period of rather steady development of theoretical physics. The framework was solid enough so that the arguments between adherents of action at a distance and adherents of proximate action by means of fields remained a rather academic discussion among physicists, although this controversy has some of the earmarks of an intuitional paradox. One should not forget, however, that throughout this period the corpuscular and wave theories of light were considered to be mutually exclusive alternatives, a viewpoint which only very much later was recognized as fallacious.

With the advent of our own century there began a period in which profound intuitional paradoxes suddenly appeared again. Those connected with the theory of relativity have been widely popularized owing perhaps to somewhat fortuitous historical circumstances. We may here merely recall the objections of A. A. Michelson, himself a leading pioneer in the experiments on which Einstein's principle of relativity is founded. Michelson objected to the concept of electromagnetic waves apart from a material ether which was the carrier of these waves; he flatly declared that he found the concept of a wave without a concretely defined carrier unacceptable. However, the main field of modern intuitional paradoxes is no doubt in quantum mechanics. The central paradox is of course that of the Heisenberg-Bohr uncertainty relations with their complementarity of the wave aspects and the corpuscular aspects of one and the same microscopic phenomenon. To illustrate the severity of the sacrifice of conventional forms of representation required here, the author may perhaps mention that in spite of a lifetime of professional work in theoretical physics he has personally been unable to develop any kind of model of complementarity, or even some substitutes for models, which he could visualize; he must rely strictly on the mathematics.

Here we come to one of the profound reasons why physical theory has in the past developed so much more thoroughly than biological theory. Although this condition is obviously in part a consequence of the greater complexity of almost all biological problems, we may now recognize that there can be little doubt that basic advance in science must often be accompanied by what we called intuitional paradoxes, sometimes mild, sometimes severe, depending on the type of problem involved. In physics, the acceptance and general intellectual assimilation of such paradoxes has been tremendously facilitated by the fact that all theories of any breadth are expressible in terms of a precise mathematical formalism that can be established once and for all. When the theory has been elaborated, therefore, the chief place where judgment and intuition enter is in the specialization of the general equations to fit a particular set of empirical conditions. Thereafter, the physicist is carried by the mathematical formalism somewhat after the manner in which a voyager is carried across a turbulent river by a boat.

3 · 7

The situation in biology appears different. We cannot of course expect any serious difficulties of interpretation so long as we remain within the realm of purely mechanistic processes, which make up such a large part of all biology. On the other hand, it would be quite surprising if in trying to establish the semi-autonomy of more comprehensive types of biological phenomena we did not encounter novel kinds of intuitional paradoxes. In particular, whenever the stability of classes goes beyond mechanistically determined feedback stabilization, information storage, etc. and involves the semi-autonomous components of organismic behavior, one may view this as representing an intuitional paradox. Remembering the purely qualitative and comparative way in which we use this term, we merely indicate thereby that there appear in biology novel abstract relationships which cannot be represented by models readily visualized in terms of more traditional concepts. There is of course little chance that the stability of classes is the only phenomenon which requires treatment in terms of non-mechanistic schemes. We may safely expect that there will be a great variety of non-mechanistic properties in biology and perhaps a related variety of intuitional paradoxes. We are picking in this book just one particular aspect of biology, the stability of classes, and are dealing with it in some detail because it seems the simplest and in some ways the most ubiquitous of the expressions of biological autonomy, of what we also called organismic behavior.

But what happens here is a modification of existing views of a somewhat different kind compared to the historical quandaries of the physicist. Broadly speaking, one might conceive of the inhomogeneity of classes of organisms as a statistical phenomenon, but it is difficult to maintain this view within the context of exact mathematics: The mathematical theory of probability can be rigorously expressed and derived from a definite set of axioms only if one defines probabilities by comparing *infinite sets* with each other. The lengthy history of the efforts to shape probability into a rigorous branch of mathematics makes it clear that the use of infinite sets is unavoidable. Hence our basic axiom, the principle of finite classes, closes the door to *rigorous, that is, purely deductive*, mathematical probability theory as an element of theoretical biology.

To illustrate this difficulty, consider the notion of randomness. Even the simplest kind of reasoning suggests that randomness is hard to define in constructive terms because the concept implies clearly the absence of any verifiable regularity. Consider a finite sequence of events: it may well happen that the application of any number of tests does not show a reasonably clearcut assurance of regularity in those events. We are then inclined to consider them as random. But assume now that this sequence is embedded as a section in an immensely larger sequence of events of the same kind. It may then well be that some of the same tests, which for the smaller set showed no appreciable evidence of regularities, give a strong indication for the presence of some regularity in the larger set. (Take as an example an extremely long and irregular sequence of digits which, however, repeats itself periodically, as happens in decimal division. If the length of the period is, say 10,000, any sub-sequence shorter than 5,000, starting at a random place but in the original order, will give no indication of periodicity.) The preceding few sentences are mere hints as to why the concept of randomness cannot be defined directly and constructively in mathematical probability theory but is introduced indirectly as a consequence of a suitable set of axioms governing the relationships of infinite sets.

If now in accordance with our principle of finite classes we limit ourselves to the comparison of finite sets, forming finite universes of discourse, an additional aspect of probability theory appears. We cannot call it a novel aspect because it has played a great role in the calculus of probabilities very nearly from its inception. We shall have to distinguish between probabilistic *deduction* and *induction*. Now, as we said, it is possible to formalize the theory of deductive probability by treating it suitably as a branch of the rigorous theory of infinite sets, but nothing of the sort is possible in a finite statistical universe. True, the distinction between finite and infinite universes of discourse is, for the scientific practitioner, essentially a matter of idealization since, practically speaking, a set of $10^{1,000}$ members is indistinguishable from an infinite set. But this idealization is yet of fundamental importance in natural philosophy, as we should now try to make clearer.

There will be no harm in recalling that science developed in conjunction with a widely felt protest against the excesses of universalistic and deductivist ideas which had been rampant through much of the history of philosophical speculation. Science, its older representative said, consists in the formulation of *part-problems* and the making of models for them which can be compared with observations. Later, as a result of the progressive successes of physical science, there arose again a tendency toward formal unification and deductivist views. In our particular context, we may identify these with a mechanistic natural philosophy.

Well known as it may be, we mention this historical background because with the introduction of quantum mechanics a new phase in this perennial problem of scientific philosophy has begun. In quantum mechanics, statistical elements are essential and cannot be eliminated. One can reduce this scheme to one of quasi-extensionality by admitting the use of infinite classes and, correspondingly, the idealization of infinitely continued processes of verification. This idealization works well enough for systems or classes which are reasonably homogeneous, because in these the replacement of a large but finite set of processes of verification by a hypothetical infinite set does not lead to serious difficulties. But if we deal with radically inhomogeneous systems or classes it becomes imperative to adopt a much more irregular universe of discourse, and this is achieved by the formal procedure of making our abstract universe large but finite. Its being large permits one to use statistical methods; its being finite prevents one from using a purely deductivist scheme. We see again, therefore, as already emphasized in Chapter 1, that we are not involved in constructing a dichotomy between "life" and "non-life" but deal with an abstract proposition of general natural philosophy, which here implies a choice between a universe of quasi-extensionality on the one hand and a much more inhomogeneous universe of discourse on the other. In the last-named we regain at least a fraction of the regularity governing the former, by virtue of the appearance of a new, logically independent concept related to stability, that of *classes*.

Probabilistic inductive inference, by its very nature, cannot be made into a rigorous, axiomatized scheme. It applies when there is given a large body of data containing statistical elements. The purpose of the inductive process is to devise a *part-model* that fits the data as closely as possible. There exists no rigorous rule of an aprioristic character, no ultimate Court of Appeal which could tell us that one model is exactly correct and other models are only more or less satisfactory approximations. There remains an element of the instructed guess, which can often be made small but cannot be eliminated altogether; hence no mathematical "rigor."

Now let us see how all this is connected with the notion of intuitional paradoxes from which we started. What we try to show is that the intuitional paradoxes which appear if we assume the semi-autonomy of biological classes do not stand by themselves, after the manner of a vitalistic doctrine; instead, they are inseparable from abstract problems that arise when probabilistic induction has to be used as an essential tool and cannot be eliminated in favor of a rigorous deductivist scheme. Now if we try to deal with semi-autonomy in a problem of theoretical biology we start from certain mechanistic components of the classes considered and use hypotheses which extend this framework on an inductive basis. Such hypotheses will involve what appear as intuitional paradoxes relative to concepts of quasi-extensionality, representing the mechanistic attitude. But since the introduction of semi-autonomy leads to the use of essentially inductive inferences which always have a certain margin of vagueness, we are not furnished with general rules that reduce those paradoxes to the interpretation of a rigorous mathematical formalism. Clearly, we are here confronted with a distinct difference in practice between theoretical physics and theoretical biology. We are to some extent thrown back upon the older views of science as being a largely inductive enterprise.

In the history of physics there have appeared from time to time extensive generalizations, such as the laws of mechanics, the laws of electrodynamics, or those of thermodynamics, which permit one to unify large areas of experience. Differential equations are established from which the solution of innumerable particular problems can be deduced by suitable specialization. If one should try, however, to combine various areas of physics under one head, a closer analysis (for instance, Tisza, 1963) shows so far little evidence that one could do so successfully. No doubt, by far the largest branch of physical science which can be subsumed under unifying principles and hence treated almost entirely by deductive methods is quantum physics. There, statistical elements are essential, but these can be taken care of, as we have seen, in a deductivist fashion by means of the idealization of an infinite universe of discourse populated by infinite homogeneous classes.

There is, however, another way of employing quantum theory with its intrinsic statistical elements, that is, by using it within an essentially finite, statistical universe, as described. From the viewpoint of formal probability theory a novel feature is now found in the fact that in such a universe deductive and inductive aspects of probability are inextricably interrelated. We can readily understand that this characteristic represents the abstract background for the concept of irreducible logical complexity. We can hardly hope to predict what direction the future development of the more mathematical analysis of this problem will take. Some simple aspects of a general statistical theory of this type may be visualized in terms of models borrowed from statistical mechanics (Elsasser, 1965) but this is only a bare beginning.

One point which emerges from these arguments is a more profound, philosophical one. A "theory of organisms," no matter how closely it fits the facts of direct observation, will not be fully satisfactory at a more fundamental level unless it embodies the valid expression of an idea so often emphasized throughout the history of biology, namely, that *organisms represent a separate form of matter:* this implies almost certainly that biological theory must be outside the dichotomy, mechanism-vitalism. It seems no accident that the generalization of quantum-mechanical concepts which becomes possible within a finite, essentially statistical universe provides just the kind of abstract framework that is needed in biological theory. In such a scheme the laws of quantum mechanics are necessary conditions which are always fulfilled but they are not sufficient determinants. It is then one of the basic expressions of irreducible logical complexity that in all cases where semi-autonomous properties of classes of organisms are involved, we shall be unable to divide the processes into a "part" which is uniquely determined by physics and another "part" which would be autonomous. An intuitional paradox of this kind appears inevitable in an organismic theory.

3 · 8

We return now from these highly abstract considerations to some matters closer to empirical biology. Let us try to guess how an observer not afflicted by modern physics would classify biological phenomena that appear to him as endowed with autonomous components. For example, he might end up by distinguishing loosely four main areas: (a) the extreme stability and the comparative uniformity of biological classes; (b) the phenomena of regeneration and healing; (c) some part of the dynamics of cerebral processes; (d) the phenomena of evolution. Mechanistic components, once they have been clearly recognized, obtrude themselves always by their comparative precision and uniformity. Thus information storage in DNA is clearly one of the mechanistic components of cellular dynamics, which subserves stability; at the other end, it seems clear enough that natural selection is the main mechanistic component of evolutionary processes. This applies even though the mechanisms involved in natural selection exhibit determinate behavior in a statistical sense only, not in the individual process. In the present work we are concentrating almost exclusively on demonstrations from category (a). So far as the partial autonomy of organismic processes is concerned, the maintenance of the uniformity of classes represents what we may well call the "conservative" aspects of autonomy. For the sake of simplicity in our argument we have, moreover, been grossly schematical. We have spoken of stationary classes that exhibit approximately uniform behavior where in nature we see almost nothing but developmental cycles. One can of course translate all our previous discussions from a universe of stationary classes into a universe of repetitive cycles. This would introduce little that is basically novel into the general structure of the theoretical scheme but would make the discussion far more involved than it need be in this context where our main purpose is to exhibit the fundamentals clearly. We trust that the reader, once he has grasped our scheme, can make the necessary adjustments and generalizations for himself.

If we look at the problem of stability from the viewpoint of developmental cycles rather than of relatively uniform classes, it turns out to have a long and remarkable history which, in fact, extends over a good deal of the history of biology itself. The invention of the microscope in the second half of the seventeenth century led to the recognition that all organisms develop out of germs. (These were of course not yet identified as cells since the cell theory was not proposed until the nineteenth century.) This discovery, superseding older notions of the "spontaneous generation" of lower organisms, led at once to the question of how information is transmitted by the germ from one generation to the next. The issue was hotly debated by two opposing schools of thought during much of the eighteenth century. The theory of *preformation* proclaimed that there is a complete replica, a miniature model of the adult, contained in every germ. The theory of *epigenesis* on the other hand, held that the germ is merely a piece of organic substance endowed with the "potential" of growing up into an adult, without precise correspondence in information content. It seems clear that these two viewpoints are intimately related to the mechanistic and vitalistic philosophies, respectively, and one could indeed identify them with these, as the author has done in his earlier book (1958).

It is readily apparent how the whole controversy arose out of a desire to describe the dynamics of development in terms of a relatively unified scheme, of one form or the other. We note the remarkable analogy with a controversy in pure physics which goes back to the same historical period: Newton, in his optics, based himself on a corpuscular theory of light, while his contemporary, Huygens, espoused a wave theory. As we know at present, the coexistence of these two categories of phenomena is essential, not only for light but also for electrons and other constituents of matter. But it might not be pure accident that these two types of dualism, in physics on the one hand and in biology on the other, developed during the same historical period and have come into the full focus of critical interest in our own time. From our viewpoint, the relationship of preformationism and epigenesis (to use here the old-fashioned terms) is at the basis of the semi-autonomy of developmental processes; it is loosely analogous to the complementarity of atomic physics. On the observational side there is indeed ample evidence in favor of each of these views of cellular dynamics. The clear-cut evidence that the DNA molecule is a storage organ for information certainly lends an altogether solid base to a somewhat modernized preformationism. On the other hand, there is the universal fact of biochemical kinetics—that all biochemical reactions proceed with a minimal dissipation of free energy—a fact that can only be interpreted by saying that the organism makes no provisions for separating "information" from "noise." The power of this argument for the epigenetic character of cellular processes has been rather overlooked in the biological literature (with notable exceptions, for instance Commoner, 1964) .

Let us, again, look at another aspect of intrinsic logical complexity in the theory of organisms. The deductive power of general principles is small for biology; it is not at all comparable to the deductive power of the principles of quantum mechanics for the properties of atoms and molecules. The semi-autonomous properties of organisms are based on the radical microscopic inhomogeneity of systems and of classes; the abstract models which embody the corresponding restriction of knowledge are those of statistical mechanics gained by proceeding from the macrovariables toward the microstates by means of inductive inferences. The restriction of knowledge implied in this depends on the specific structural character of the inhomogeneities. This may vary from class to class, and there can be few generalizations—thus verifying again our previous proposition that the autonomy of biological classes is invariably only *semi*-autonomy.

Nothing would be further from the truth than to construe this state of affairs as an impoverishment of the power of scientific method in biology. What it says is that biological investigations can never be as abstractly universal as are most physical theories; biology is likely to remain in the future, as it is at present, a vastly more empirical enterprise, tied more closely to particular classes of phenomena. Cellular dynamics, ecology, and other fields in which quantitative methods are applicable are undoubtedly only in their beginning as branches of theoretical science. The recent, remarkable study by Goodwin (1963) on the theory of non-linear chemical oscillations in the cell gives a glimpse of the vast areas of theoretical investigation that are still wide open and unexplored. We should be clear, however, about the fact that the pursuit of such analysis along purely mechanistic lines must have its intrinsic limitations, and that modifications resulting from the semi-autonomous character of biological phenomena will sooner or later have to come into play.

We propose to digress here briefly into a matter of terminology. The term "preformation" is rather obsolete and may safely be replaced by mechanistic behavior or mechanistic components, as we have done above. On the other hand, the term "epigenesis" and the adjective "epigenetic," are still in common use among biologists. We think that within the framework of the present theory the term "epigenetic" may be used essentially as a synonym for the semi-autonomous components of developmental processes. In his earlier book the author introduced the term "biotonic" to designate all those biological processes that exhibit strong aspects of autonomy. We have abandoned the use of this term, largely because it seems to have evoked vitalistic connotations; it might make it appear as if autonomous features of organisms could be discussed by themselves and analyzed on general principles, apart from the organism's mechanistic structures to which they are related. This, as we have seen, would be a grave error.

3 · 9

As we had occasion to observe in Section 3.7, the much more rigorous structure of physical science as compared to the looser structure of biology is an essential aspect of our theoretical scheme. Let us as an example compare the vagueness of deductions from purely biological principles with the sharpness of deductive specializations that commonly occur in physics and chemistry. Consider a water molecule (in the gaseous state). It is characterized by the mass of the oxygen nucleus and the masses of the two protons, by the charges of these particles, and the number, mass, and charge of the electrons needed for electrical neutralization. Inserting these quantities (half a dozen or so numbers) into the Schrödinger equation, which governs all atomic and molecular systems, it becomes possible to calculate with almost any accuracy desired the frequencies of literally thousands of observable spectral lines of the molecule. The example is by no means overly artifical because many calculations of a type not at all remote from this ideal have been carried out, leaving no doubt at all that, given enough computational facilities, exhaustive calculations of the sort are altogether feasible.

To turn to biology, the deductive inferences drawn from its general principles appear to be "weak" throughout. The idea that the structure of biology is comparatively loose has of course been eloquently expressed before. J. T. Bonner (1960) has recalled the absence of truly general principles applying to developmental processes; he indicates that this state of affairs might well correspond to an intrinsic rather than just a temporary (or shall we say, contemporary) ignorance. Bonner remarks furthermore on the widespread feeling among embryologists and other students of development that while our knowledge of detailed processes is steadily on the increase, there seems to be no evidence that some unifying principle has emerged or can be perceived on the horizon.

When it comes to evolution, matters are even more intricate. The fact of evolution is the one monumental, unifying principle in biology. However, on dealing with the nature of the processes involved in evolution we find that matters have become far more complicated since the classical period of Darwin and his immediate successors. According to recent comprehensive works (Simpson, 1953; Mayr, 1963) the conditions that are conducive to evolution are intricate, multiple, and often variable; Simpson says that the only statement which can be asserted is that the gene pool of a population is subject to unidirectional variation as time goes on. He calls this variation "selection" (p. 138), but at the same time he emphasizes very strongly that the various selective agencies are almost never uniquely determined, which leaves the theoretical problem still essentially open.

We are here interested in these subjects only insofar as they may be able to shed light on the question of whether there is empirical evidence for any kind of universal biological law. Here we note that one of the outstanding generalizations of the early days after the Darwinian revolution was the so-called biogenetic law, whose main proponent was E. Häckel. According to this law, the embryonic development of the individual is a shortened recapitulation of the evolutionary transformations that have led to the formation of the species. In the century which has intervened since, a vast amount of research work has been done, which has brought to light the ever-increasing complexity of the evolutionary as well as the developmental processes involved. In an admirably concise book, De Beer (1958) has surveyed the evidence and comes to the flat conclusion that there is not enough regularity left to speak of the existence of such a law.

Furthermore, there are to all practical intents and purposes no general regularities in taxonomy except for a few specific adaptive ones which can hardly be claimed to be specializations of some general vital principle. It is, moreover, a rather frequent experience in physiology that when, after many years, sometimes decades, of hard work, the investigators have arrived at a reasonably coherent and intelligent scheme, a succeeding generation finds that the original scheme has been too simple and that the real conditions are much more complicated than had ever been expected. This seems to have happened in the study of the metabolic pathways for instance. Several other instances are found in nerve physiology: in the analysis of synaptic action, the connectivity of nerve nets, and the flow pattern of nervous impulses. An experienced physiologist could readily multiply these examples.

3 · 10

Again, there is one type of regularity or law in biology which, while not perhaps universal, is so extremely widespread and at the same time precise that in this it resembles the laws of physics. The prototype of such a quantitative relationship is found in Mendel's laws. They hold whenever sexual reproduction takes place. The precision of Mendel's laws is the reason that genetics has so much more the character of an exact science than other branches of biology which also deal with the living organism in its complexity. Now at the present stage of our knowledge there can no longer be any doubt that these laws are a direct reflection of certain underlying molecular properties. We know what the latter are, of course: they have to do with the very precise processes of doubling the strands of DNA during mitosis and of their separation into two halves that occurs in the process of meiosis. It does not follow from this that the phenotypical changes which result are, in a reductionist fashion, *uniquely* determined by the molecular properties of DNA. Indeed somewhere between the genetic molecular material and the phenotype, epigenetic components ought to intervene if their presence is essential.

Another example of a quantitative regularity that readily comes to mind is Fechner's law, which says that for any sense organ the strength of sensory perception (that is, the intensity of the signal travelling to the brain through the afferent nerves) is proportional to the logarithm of the external stimulus impinging on the sense organ. There are numerous verifications of this law for practically every sense known. One cannot doubt that this law is the expression of a specific but widespread mechanism for the transformation of sensory stimulation into sequences of nerve impulses. Any competent physiologist could easily enumerate many similar cases of regularities where the mechanisms are so delicate that certain quantitative laws become apparent before the molecular processes have been understood in detail. The vast field of photosynthesis offers abundant examples. Needless to say, when dealing with grossly macroscopic phenomena one cannot speak of a difference at all in any analysis based on the laws of physics and chemistry, as between an organism and an inorganic body. In such cases the models of statistical mechanics furnish unambiguously defined *averages* which are independent of the microscopic details of the model; these averages simply follow laws expressed in macroscopic physical regularities.

Recently, H. Morowitz (1966) has made an extensive

survey of those structural and dynamical facts which are common to all organisms and which therefore may be claimed to constitute representative biological generalizations. This survey begins with certain facts of chemistry. There is a set of small organic molecules (of molecular weight up to 500, say) which is found in all organisms, and a much more extensive set found in many but not all of them. Next, when it comes to large molecules, all organisms seem to store genetic commands in DNA molecules, and furthermore the well known DNA-RNA-protein process of transformation and duplication appears to be common to all living systems. Next, life seems to have settled upon one dominant process for the utilization of concentrated chemical energy, the hydrolysis of high-energy phosphate bonds.

While these facts are primarily chemical, some others refer to structures larger than a molecule. All organisms either are cells or are composed of cells. All cells have ribosomes consisting of about equal parts of protein and RNA, which are the loci of protein synthesis. Finally, wherever membranes appear (and they are of course one of the principal working tools of the organism) they seem to have a rather uniform composition, structure, and thickness.

Even a superficial survey of this list indicates that the *engineering* aspects of biology here dominate the picture completely—if we are permitted to apply the term engineering in an obvious sense to the mechanics of organisms and if we agree for simplicity to designate the construction of complicated organic molecules as a form of engineering. Clearly, certain aspects of the structure and dynamics of molecular organization have proved sufficiently superior to those of competitive forms that the latter, if they once existed, are now no longer about. There is nowhere the slightest indication that, in dealing with biological generalizations of this type, any general principle of a purely biological nature, going beyond physics, chemistry, and engineering, is involved.

3 · 11

We are now coming to the end of our brief survey of the conceptual structure and the abstract assumptions that must underlie a biological theory in which organisms are *semi*-autonomous dynamical systems. While these considerations have been very general, we have had at the back of our minds mainly the model of a cell as an integrated biochemical system, with little regard to the peculiar and novel complexities that appear in higher organisms. Owing to this limitation of our program we have had to ignore a phenomenon which is altogether basic in the biology of higher organisms, namely, the existence of *hierarchies* of order. We have encountered it so far only marginally, in the comments of P. Weiss reproduced in Section 1.21. There is, again, no rigorous scheme of hierarchical order, but we might, in textbook-like fashion, enumerate the following sequence just as an example: molecule, organelle, cell, tissue, organ, multicellular organism, society. This series is not meant as a prototype but merely as one exhibit of multiple schemes which are capable of an almost endless number of variants, condensations, or extensions. The existence of such hierarchies is a patent fact of immediate biological observation; it is certainly not just an abstract deduction from the analysis of complicated data.

If our basic theoretical scheme is correct we may expect that in each case there is a greater degree of invariance (as P. Weiss puts it), or order, at any higher level than might appear compatible on a superficial view with the inhomogeneity of components at correspondingly lower levels. The study or even the survey of hierarchies is beyond our present scope. It is also hardly likely to yield laws or principles of a very general nature, for reasons which have already been exhibited in our preceding discussion. What we wish to emphasize is that the assumption of a finite universe of discourse containing radically inhomogeneous classes seems to provide a suitable abstract understructure within which the existence of hierarchies in biology can be conceived, whereas the traditional, relatively more rigorous and inflexible logic and formalism of physical science appears rather powerless in the face of these phenomena. Any attempt at formalization of the concept of hierarchies of order or classes within the usual framework of mathematical abstractions with its infinities is likely to be unrealistic and in consequence more or less impractical. It cannot, in general, render account of the characteristic interpenetration of effects pertaining to various levels which is made possible by the ubiquitous presence of inhomogeneity. This state of affairs implies a failure to find definite binary answers to questions regarding classes of phenomena, questions which might in other circumstances seem straightforward enough.

A further concept inextricably related with the preceding ideas, and necessary for their understanding, is that of *individuality*. We may define individuality in a purely formal manner by saying that it represents the actual existence of a configuration (or of a process) which is an immensely rare occurrence if viewed abstractly against an immense number of possible configurations (or processes). Again, the paramount role of individuality in higher organisms is a patent fact of observation, not just a theoretical subtlety. The highest degree of individuality prevails of course in cerebral functions of humans (mind, higher emotions, etc.), but pronounced individuality exists in very numerous if not in most anatomical and physiological characteristics of higher organisms. A popular example from anatomy is the variety of fingerprints; another example taken from physiology is the variety of blood groups. If all the subgroups of these which can be found by sufficiently refined methods are counted, the set of possible combinations vastly exceeds the number of human beings. Another, rather spectacular example is what Williams (1956) has called "biochemical individuality," having to do with the almost incredible variability in the concentrations of numerous chemical compounds from one individual to the next. Every medical man and every naturalist knows a great deal about the tremendous anatomical and physiological variability of all higher organisms. It is easy to show by simple calculations that if we allow a certain variability of a reasonably large number of parameters, then the number of different individuals compatible with this is invariably immense, so that the preceding formal definition of individuality applies.

It follows furthermore from the last-named definition that individuality is a universal property of organisms. We can see here the practical importance of the principle of finite classes: it allows us to introduce the concept of individuality (as well as hierarchy, of course) into biology in a reasonably well-defined and essentially formal manner. At the lowest organizational level, however —that of biochemical dynamics—individuality is *potential*, in the sense that the precise microstate of an organism cannot be ascertained. What remains at this level is the numerical relationship between the number of possible microstates and the number of actual members of the class, the former being immense compared to the latter. What we are left with, therefore, at this level, are essentially all the operational and practical consequences of individuality; what we are losing, in part at least, is the possibility of ascertaining structural individuality by direct inspection of the object. To some extent this remains true for all organisms, because all organisms are in the last resort critically dependent on such biochemistry; but as we go to larger and also more complexly structured organisms, there are more and more macroscopic parameters with respect to which individuality can be clearly exhibited and demonstrated.

It is not much of a generalization to say that individuality clearly increases as one rises on the evolutionary scale. One might even use individuality broadly as a measure of evolutionary advance. Man is then the "highest" of organisms quite simply because men, due to the complexity of their brains, can exhibit a vastly higher degree of individuality than any other kind of organism. In this context one should consistently keep in mind the idea of intrinsic logical complexity. There is no reason to assume that the old Darwinian measure of evolutionary advance in terms of adaptation becomes false and should be thrown out. What we are confronted with is not a binary situation, an either-or question which would give rise to "two opposed schools of thought." We have no basis for thinking that there is a single criterion for evolutionary advance, just as there is not just a single criterion for so many other legitimate questions in the life sciences. Are there biological questions to which precise, uniquely determined answers can be given? They must be rare indeed. We see then that to introduce irreducible logical complexity on a purely abstract basis, as we have done here, brings us much closer to the preoccupations of the naturalist than we are in the absence of this idea, and it separates us to some extent from the more rigorous methods of the physical scientist. Anybody who deals with these fields, in addition to being a scientist, should have some capabilities of intuition, perhaps on occasion a little of the poet in him, if he is to apprehend clearly the intricate marvels of Creation.

REFERENCES

Bernard, Claude. 1878. *La Science expérimentale*, Paris. For Bernard's general philosophical attitudes see also an English translation: *An Introduction to the Study of Experimental Medicine*, Paperback edition, Dover, New York, 1957.

Bohr, Niels. 1933. *Nature* 131: 421-423, 457-459; see also *Atomic Physics and the Description of Nature*, Cambridge University Press, 1934; *Atomic Physics and Human Knowledge*, John Wiley, New York, 1958.

Bonner, John Tyler. 1960. *American Scientist* 48:514-527.

Brillouin, Leon. 1964. *Scientific Uncertainty and Information*, Academic Press, New York.

Commoner, Barry. 1964a. *Nature* 202:960-968.

———— 1964b. *American Scientist* 52:365-387.

De Beer, Sir Gavin. 1958. *Embryos and Ancestors*, 3rd edn., Clarendon Press, Oxford.

Elsasser, Walter M. 1958. *The Physical Foundation of Biology*, Pergamon Press, New York and London.

———— 1962a. *Zeitschrift für Physik* 171:66-82.

———— 1962b. *Journal of Theoretical Biology* 3:164-191. See also *ibid.* 1 (1961):27-58; 4 (1963):166-174; 7 (1964):53-67.

———— 1965. *Proceedings of the National Academy of Sciences, U.S.* 54:1431-1436.

Frey-Wyssling, Albert. 1953. *Submicroscopic Morphology of Protoplasm*, 2nd edn., Elsevier Publ. Co., Amsterdam and Houston.

Gerard, R. W., ed. 1958. "Concepts of Biology," *Behavioral Science* Vol. 3, No. 2 (April); reproduced as Publication 560 of the National Academy of Science–National Research Council; available through their Publications Office.

REFERENCES

Goodwin, Brian C. 1963. *Temporal Organization in Cells*, Academic Press, New York.

Jordan, Pascual. 1948. *Die Physik und das Geheimnis des organischen Lebens*, 6th edn., F. Vieweg & Sohn, Braunschweig.

Mayr, Ernst. 1963. *Animal Species and Evolution*, Harvard University Press, Cambridge, Mass.

Morowitz, Harold. 1966. To appear in *Progress in Theoretical Biology*, F. Snell, ed., Vol. 1, Academic Press, New York.

Pollard, Ernest C. 1965. *American Scientist* 53:437-463.

Simpson, George Gaylord. 1953. *The Major Features of Evolution*, Columbia University Press, New York.

Tisza, Laszlo. 1963. *Reviews of Modern Physics* 35:151-185.

Von Bertalanffy, Ludwig. 1952. *Problems of Life*, C. A. Watts & Co., London. (Paperback reprint, Harper Torchbooks, New York, 1960.)

Von Neumann, J. 1933. *Mathematische Grundlagen der Quantenmechanik*, Springer, Berlin. (English translation: *Mathematical Foundations of Quantum Mechanics*, Princeton University Press, Princeton, 1955.)

——— 1956. In *Automata Studies*, C. E. Shannon and J. McCarthy, eds., Princeton University Press, Princeton, pp. 42-98.

Waddington, C. H. 1961. *The Nature of Life*, George Allen & Unwin, London (Atheneum, New York, 1962).

Whitehead, Alfred North. 1957. *The Concept of Nature*, Chapter 2. Paperback reprint, University of Michigan Press, Ann Arbor.

Williams, Roger J. 1956. *Biochemical Individuality*, John Wiley, New York.

Winograd, S., and Cowan, J. D. 1963. *Reliable Computation in the Presence of Noise*, M.I.T. Press, Cambridge, Mass.

INDEX

Bold-face type indicates definitions or chief descriptions